DRESS FOR SUCCESS

DRESS FOR SUCCESS

by

JOHN T. MOLLOY

WARNER BOOKS

A Warner Communications Company

To my best friend, Maureen

WARNER BOOKS EDITION

Library of Congress Catalog Card Number: 75-7647

ISBN 0-446-38263-9 (U.S.A.)
ISBN 0-446-38264-7 (Canada)

This Warner Books Edition is published by arrangement with
Peter H. Wyden/Publisher

Cover design by Gene Light

Cover photograph by Jerry West

Warner Books, Inc., 666 Fifth Avenue, New York, N.Y.
10103

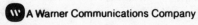 A Warner Communications Company

Printed in the United States of America

First Printing: September, 1978

15   14   13   12   11

TABLE OF CONTENTS

INTRODUCTION:
WHY MEN DRESS
FOR FAILURE AND
WHAT TO DO ABOUT IT

FACT: Most American men dress for failure. They do so because they make one or more of four suicidal mistakes: They let their wives or girlfriends choose their clothing. They let their favorite sales clerks choose their clothing. They let designers and "fashion consultants" choose their clothing. Or they let their backgrounds choose their clothing.

There is a way to avoid making any of those mistakes and to dress for success instead. *Let research choose your clothing.* My research is unique in concept, scope and results. It has been conducted over a period of fifteen years and includes the opinions and subconscious reactions of over 15,000 executives in all phases of business, as well as those of a wide cross section of the general public.

This research is based on the very reasonable premise that the two great behaviorists Pavlov and Skinner are right: We are preconditioned by our environment, and the clothing we wear is an integral part of that environment. The way we dress has remarkable impact on the people we meet professionally or socially and greatly (sometimes crucially) affects how they treat us.

It is possible, through the skillful manipulation of dress in any particular situation, to evoke a favorable response to your personality and your needs.

And it is possible for me, based on the research I have done, to teach you to dress for success.

I do not ask you to accept these conclusions immediately; I do hope that you will accept them when you have finished this book.

I will never ask you to concede that it is fair or just or moral for a man's success or failure to depend, to a large extent, on how he dresses. But that is very much the way the money-oriented sectors of our culture work; and it is my contention that in matters of individual striving, it is far more rewarding to let reality be your guide, to use the system rather than ignore or flout it.

Many critics may charge that my approach to successful dress is snobbish, conservative, bland and conformist. They may further charge that I am encouraging the executive herd-instinct. To these charges, I must plead guilty, for my research documents that, in matters of clothing, conservative, class-conscious conformity is absolutely essential to the individual success of the American business and professional man. Executives in particular do constitute a herd, and those who understand how to cope rather than fight are much more likely to emerge as leaders than as casualties.

FACT: People who look successful and well educated receive preferential treatment in almost all of their social or business encounters. And since I came to the conclusion long ago that every man wishes to be treated as if he is important, I assumed that the reason why most men do not dress in a manner that commands respect is money, or the lack thereof. Later, when I became involved in research that proved that money is not the issue, and that, with a little care and effort, the average man can easily create the look of success, I attempted to find out why he does not make that attempt. Then I discovered the four villains listed at the very outset of this chapter.

2

Introduction: Why Men Dress for Failure

WHY WOMEN FAIL THEIR MEN

I realize that a large number of women are now screaming to themselves, "I am not a villain. I love my husband and always want him to look good."

Certainly, women are not conscious villains, but the result of their efforts is the same. The fact is that for years women have been indoctrinated by the fashion industry to believe that anything new, up-to-date, innovative and different is desirable. Most women, regardless of their status, would like to be leaders in fashion, and they transfer this desire to their husbands when they choose or influence their husbands' selection of clothing. They want their husbands to look good to *them,* and time and again they select a garment that is fashionable in the female sense of the word. Unfortunately the reality—that is, the attitude of the American corporate establishment—militates almost totally against such a look for top executives.

My evidence is overwhelming. In one survey I conducted, 92 percent of the executives who were questioned said they would not hire a man who presented himself for a job interview wearing high-fashion clothing. In another survey, 87 percent of the executives questioned said they would reprove any subordinate who continually dressed in that manner.

If any doubting Thomasinas are reading this, I can only ask that they visit any top-league executive office and look around, making careful mental notes on how the men are dressed. Then these women should ask themselves a question that could be worth a lot more than $64,000 to their husbands' careers: "Would my husband, dressed in the clothes I have chosen for him, fit in with these successful men?"

Most women would be forced to answer no.

HOW SALESMEN SABOTAGE THEIR CUSTOMERS

The next group that leads men down the path to sartorial slaughter are sales clerks. I mean no offense, and there are certainly some qualified exceptions, but most men's clothing store salesmen come from limited backgrounds and possess limited education, limited personal resources and limited knowledge of the business world. Little or no formal training is required for the job, and even the major stores that do have training programs generally teach their employees how to sell, rather than how to serve.

Their job is to move the merchandise they have, not to provide you with the clothing you should be wearing. If they did know what you should be wearing, they would not be in the relatively menial positions that they're locked into. Don't let them lock you into the position *you're* in.

WHY FASHION DESIGNERS ARE DANGEROUS

The final villain who can be personified is the fashion designer or consultant. A designer's name on a garment is supposed to represent quality and good taste. But more often than not, all a designer's label on a garment means is that he is getting a slice of the take. Even when quality is present, it is usually accompanied by an exorbitant price and foreign design, neither of which should be an inducement to buy.

The trouble with fashion designers, many of whom come from Rome, is that they do not export the maxim, "When in Rome, do as the Romans do." They ignore the fact that America is largely run by men who dress in a specific, traditional way, and they imply that we are all tasteless peasants who must be guided for our own good. Their condescension is not only insulting, it is also stupid. It is evident from the statistics I have already cited that a high fashion look is rejected by the American business establishment—the very men whose clothing budgets could make designers richer than they ever dreamed, if only they would design clothes suited to people's needs, rather than clothing that feeds their own egos.

There are, of course, some fashion designers and consultants who are American. But male fashion designing was not exactly a chic profession in this country until very recently. Consequently these men are, by and large, products of the lower-middle class, and regardless of their income, their lower-middle-class taste lingers on.

Although fashion designers have been responsible for many positive changes in men's clothing in recent years, and some liberalization of styles, patterns and colors has taken place, this trend is basically confined to leisure wear. For corporate and professional clothing, the loudly proclaimed radical changes in acceptability are more fashion fantasy than business fact. The truth is that business styles change with glacierlike slowness, and there is no point in risking career, income and social position by gambling on passing (and very expensive) fads. The only men's bank accounts that are fattened by a new fad are those of the designer and manufacturer who created it.

Even if designer clothes reflect quality and sophistication, as some very definitely do, the seductive manipulations of most fashion designers should still be viewed with suspicion, and for a more fundamental reason. They are advisors and associates of the manufacturer, not of the buyer. And their best interests are not necessarily his.

I am the consumer's man. My interests are his because I like it that way and because it is he who pays me. My interest in clothing begins where that of the designer, the manufacturer, the retailer and his clerks leave off—at the point of sale. For a decade and a half, I have thoroughly researched what effect clothing has after the buyer puts it on. Through this research, I am able to engineer a man's wardrobe to elicit just about any desired effect.

WHAT RESEARCH CAN DO FOR YOU

I can help you look successful, fatherly, honest, sexy, or even use clothing to mask or overcome detrimental physical characteristics or quirks. I have successfully applied these techniques on behalf of national political figures of both parties, executives

5

of many of America's leading corporations, diplomats of foreign governments stationed in the United States, foreign executives seeking to do business here, television personalities, salesmen, courtroom lawyers, defendants in major criminal trials, professional associations, and, of course, private individuals.

GETTING DOWN TO CASES

ITEM: A few years ago, a Midwestern politician running for a minor office called me in as a consultant when the political pros told him he had no chance of achieving even that lowly position because he lacked charisma. I changed his dress and his image and he is today governor of his state.

ITEM: I regularly consult with a major New York law firm and dress the young lawyers when they are hired. For the first six months to a year of their employment, I conduct a seminar for them on effective dress in and out of the courtroom. After one of these seminars, during which I had casually and somewhat playfully mentioned that a man could be made to look sexy, one of the young men stayed behind to ask if I would help him. He didn't want to become a swinger, he said, but wanted to settle down and get married. The problem was that he wasn't at all successful with women. I gave him copies of my research on what clothing appeals to women, and didn't see him again for about a year. When I did see him, I asked if my research had helped.

"Yes," was his emphatic and cheerful reply, "so much that I no longer want to get married."

ITEM: About six months ago, I was hired by an accounting firm to establish a dress code for their accountants who did audits in their clients' offices. Several of the senior partners of the firm pointed out an employee to me. They said he was a brilliant accountant, but dressed so badly that they just couldn't send him out to important clients. He did dress very poorly, and even though he had received strong hints to change his ways, he ignored them. Unless he changed soon, he was on his way out, rather than up. I had a short, frank talk with him, but he resolutely refused to believe that clothing would make any difference to his career.

Going back to the senior partners, I said, "Look, if I can get him to dress correctly, at least when he goes out on business, will you give him several important clients?" They agreed, and I finally was able to persuade him to follow my advice just as a test. I think he really only went along to get me off his back.

Only six months later, his salary had been increased by $12,000 a year; his clients couldn't have been happier with him; and he was well on his way to becoming a partner in the firm. I now choose all his clothing and have a three-year contract with him.

ITEM: Several years ago, I was approached by a self-made millionaire. Here was a man who had pulled himself up from poverty and achieved the American dream—except that for him and his family it had become a nightmare. He had moved into a wealthy, sophisticated suburb of New York, and he had the money to buy most of his neighbors and give them to charity with no significant effect on his bank balance. But the neighbors did have some assets that his money could not buy—class, education and sophistication. It was not so much that the neighbors were nasty or snobbish, but more that they had nothing in common with these products of the lower classes. His wife and children had no neighborhood friends. They were lonely and the children were failing in school.

In this millionaire's case, dress was not enough to overcome his massive social problems. But it was the starting point for him and his entire family. Once I had them looking like their neighbors, we set about getting him and his wife into night courses where they acquired the cultural refinements they needed to talk with their neighbors on an equal footing. Today, they are one of the most respected and best-liked families in the community.

HOW TO OVERCOME YOUR OWN BACKGROUND

As in the case of the lonely millionaire, helping people to handle their own backgrounds, that great impersonal killer of

7

careers, has always been my primary goal. In twentieth-century America, this is particularly difficult to achieve because most of us forget that when the founding fathers declared that all men are created equal, they did not mean that we are literally born into equal environments. Democratically but foolishly, we bristle at the concept of training a man to move from one class to another and dismiss this need as a nineteenth-century Dickensian notion. Unrealistically, we expect the mere acquisition of position and money to move men socially. We try to ignore the fact that people who possess wealth and education, our great social yardsticks, do carry themselves differently and do set themselves apart from their poorer, less-educated neighbors by distinctive patterns of speech and dress.

Successful dress is really no more than achieving good taste and the look of the upper-middle class, or whatever is perceived by the greatest number of people to reflect these qualities. Historically, in Europe, there were men and organizations who taught the upwardly mobile man how to acquire the necessary manners and taste of the class to which he aspired. When these Pygmalions came to America, they moved into the world of fashion, but generally treated America as a country without classes and without class. Neither conclusion is correct, and so their input was of no value.

WHY SUCCESSFUL DRESS IS NOT EXPENSIVE

My input would be just as valueless if cost were the only factor in determining the socioeconomic associations that are evoked by clothing, because the bottom line would always be how much money a man has to spend. In fact, upper-middle-class shades of color and patterns and textures have been available in relatively inexpensive clothing for years. With the improved technical abilities achieved by the clothing industry in recent years, you can get at moderate prices almost all the variations of color, pattern and texture that were once the exclusive province of the upper-middle-class man. If a man knows how to choose his clothing—and after you finish this book you will—he can, without substantial increase in his clothing expenditure, look right on all occasions.

With a very simple set of do's and don'ts that it took me years to devise, it is now possible for any man to look like a success and greatly improve his chances for becoming one.

Naturally, successful dress cannot put a boob in the board room, but incorrect dress can definitely keep an intelligent, able man out.

The first rule of dress is common sense. This means that if you are a Wall Street stockbroker, you would be wise to go to work in a conservative, three-piece pinstripe suit. If you're an art director in a Madison Avenue ad agency, a television talk show personality, or any man working in any so-called "glamour industry," you would be wise to avoid conservative clothing in favor of more flamboyant, fashionable and "with-it" gear.

Not only individuals, but industries, professions, specific jobs, geography and climate dictate a natural clothing range that is easily identified through common sense. Particular situations can dictate their own clothing rules. For example, if your boss never went to college and hates anyone who walks, talks and looks as if he did, it would be wise to avoid the Ivy League look. If you live in California or Florida, naturally you do not wear the heavy flannel suits common in most other areas of the country. You wear lighter, brighter colors, for reasons of comfort if no other. In short, although this book is filled with rules, not every rule can work for every man in every situation or locality. Every rule must be measured against every individual's own specific circumstances and adapted accordingly.

So while this book certainly cannot do all things for all people, it can:

• Open the doors to the executive suite to men for whom they are now closed.

• Make movement up the social ladder easier for some.

• Make it easier for many men to sell everything better—including themselves.

- Make the right wardrobe less expensive.
- Give women a simple, sensible guide to buying men's clothing.
- Teach men how women like them to dress.
- Permanently change the way men look at clothing.
- Make a large number of people in the fashion industry angry as hell.

1.

A TWENTIETH-CENTURY APPROACH TO MEN'S CLOTHING

If you asked me to divide the history of the world into two time periods, I would set the break early in the seventeenth century —when Francis Bacon introduced the scientific method. Before then, doctors commonly bled the sick. It was not that doctors were stupid, rather, it was just as easy for them to argue logically for bleeding people as it was to argue against. Neither argument was confused by any facts based on research.

Once Bacon's method of observation, deduction and induction was applied to medicine, the conclusion that bleeding the sick was usually more harmful than helpful became inescapable. The application of the scientific method made it inevitable that sooner or later men would land on the moon, that hearts would be transplanted, and that in the future cancer will be conquered. It was also inevitable that someone would come along and apply valid scientific research methods to dress and its effects.

Those of you who are, at this point, saying that fashion is an art form and not a science are making the same kind of statement as the eighteenth-century doctors who continued to bleed people. I do not contend that fashion is an absolute science, but I know that conscious and unconscious attitudes toward dress can be measured and that this measurement will aid men in making valid judgments about the way they dress.

After all, if we look at the reasons why man puts on clothing, there are only three: to protect himself from the elements; to obey whatever his laws of modesty happen to be; and to look "good" to the people around him, or to the people he's going to meet, or to the world in general. And when we say that clothing can make a man look "good," we are really saying that it makes him look authoritative, powerful, rich, responsible, reliable, friendly, masculine or any other trait that is meaningful to us and meets with our approval.

There are men in the fashion industry who try very hard to make men look "good." We know they are trying hard because their livelihoods depend on their success. But like medical men prior to the scientific method, their attempts are made ineffective because they use subjective methods. A designer sits alone in a room and decides that a particular garment will make men look good. He does not bother to ask other men their opinions of the garment; he does not measure what the world thinks of it. He does not apply any scientific principles to arrive at his decision, and therefore his judgment has all the validity of the seventeenth-century doctors' judgment: it is articulate; it can be systematized; it can be defended in all ways except before the avalanche of evidence. And I believe that this book is the first rumble of that avalanche.

Before going further, I think it is important to explain how I came to conduct experiments in fashion. I should like, of course, to claim insight, brilliance, even genius. I cannot. I was forced into it.

Fifteen years ago, I was a young English teacher at a prep school in Stamford, Connecticut. The job paid badly, and after my first year I knew I couldn't afford to stay on. The owner of the school, wanting me to stay but knowing my economic problems, offered to find me a part-time job to supplement my income. I agreed, and that summer worked with a group of teachers who had received government funding to give remedial instruction to needy children in Connecticut and to do general research in education.

As my research project, I chose the effects of clothing on learning in the classroom. I was somewhat surprised when the idea was approved and I was given the go ahead to undertake the study. I was also a bit frightened, because I was not at all qualified to conduct research of any type. But, needing the money, I immediately ran to the library and began reading everything I could find about research methods.

The outcome was that I conducted a series of experiments in Connecticut schools and proved that the clothing worn by the teachers substantially affected the work and attitudes of pupils. This was demonstrated in one case by two teachers who taught the same class in separate half-day sessions. One of the teachers wore rather casual clothing—penny loafers, a tie slightly open at the collar—while the other wore traditional lace shoes, always black, a conservative suit and a conservative tie. The students worked longer and harder for the teacher with the old-fashioned look.

Just at the time of my discovery, research funds were cut back by the government, and my project should have come to a halt. But I was hooked and started taking courses and doing research on my own. At the end of one year, I believed I had accomplished a breakthrough in education. In my report, I showed that clothing had a significant affect on discipline, work habits and attitudes in the classroom and that at different socioeconomic levels the pupils responded differently to various types of clothing.

When I took my report to my educator bosses, however, I was told that since the experiment was over, the report was not needed and that even if my results were valid, they wouldn't know what to do with them. Frustrated and dismayed, I filed away my report and went on about my business as a teacher. But I was not to escape from my research quite so easily.

The following summer, again needing work, I applied for a

part-time job at an elegant, expensive Fifth Avenue clothing store. The interviewer asked how much I knew about clothing. After I had described my research project, I was immediately assigned the task of coordinating the clothing purchased by the members of several law firms that sent all their members to the store.

I expected some difficulty in helping the lawyers, because I never met them. I would receive only a name attached to a suit that needed a shirt and tie to be matched with it. The complaints I received—and there were many—never argued with my ability to coordinate clothing, but were related to the appropriateness of a given outfit for a member of the legal profession.

Since there was no consistency to the complaints, I was puzzled and therefore wrote, in the name of my employer, to several of my biggest clients. I told them I had noticed their members were making judgments about clothing that I felt were invalid. I also included some background information on the experiments I had conducted in the classroom, where credibility is as much a factor as it is in the courtroom. I also offered to meet with a member of each firm and discuss what I thought was proper attire for a lawyer in the courtroom.

All of our clients accepted my offer, and we were getting along famously when the store discovered that I was giving the extra service and decided to charge the firms accordingly—but without giving me a raise. I became annoyed, then angry, and quit. To my delight, the law firms engaged me directly for my services and began spreading the word that I was a valuable man to know.

At that point, twelve years ago, I became America's first wardrobe engineer.

Dress for Success is intended as a practical tool, not as an academic exercise. I am not (and you are not) interested in theory for its own sake. We will leave that to the educators. If I were to describe the methodology and results of all my experiments, surveys and tests in order to substantiate every statement in this book, it would run several thousand pages and be absolutely useless. I will spare you that, but for those with backgrounds in research, I should state that I followed standard research techniques with several exceptions. There was virtually no review of the literature in the field, since there is no literature in the field. At the stage of creating a hypothesis, I refrained from making a researcher's prediction unless it had to be included in the formal statement of the hypothesis (these predictions can become self-fulfilling prophecies, I believe).

When designing the data-gathering instrument, I often had to limit my objective since I found that corporations were unwisely frugal when appropriating funds for this essential work. But I can state that I never undertook a new project without testing and retesting the reliability of the testing instrument, and the only validity I considered adequate was predictive validity. While this is the validity measure that is least often used in the social disciplines, it is by far the best. Naturally, I ran pilot projects when needed and set up control groups whenever possible.

I am now going to present a few examples of my research in a way that will make them clear to any reader who will bear with me, and will offer no more technical jargon.

THE PROOF: WHAT WORKS AND WHAT DOESN'T

Since I had very early on discovered that the socioeconomic value of a man's clothing is important in determining his credibility with certain groups, his ability to attract certain kinds of women and his acceptance to the business community, one of the first elements I undertook to research was the socioeconomic level of all items of clothing.

Take the raincoat, for example. Most raincoats sold in this country are either beige or black; those are the two standard colors. Intuitively I felt that the beige raincoat was worn generally by the upper-middle class and black by the lower-middle class.

First I visited several Fifth Avenue stores that cater almost exclusively to upper-middle-class customers and attempted to ascertain the number of beige raincoats versus black raincoats being sold. The statistical breakdown was approximately four to one in favor of beige. I then checked stores on the lower-middle-class level and found that almost the reverse statistic applied. They sold four black raincoats to each beige raincoat.

This indicated that in all probability my feeling was correct, but recognizing that there were many variables that could discredit such preliminary research, I set the second stage in motion. On rainy days, I hired responsible college students to stand outside subway stations in determinable lower-middle-class neighborhoods and outside determinable upper-middle-class suburban commuter-stations, all in the New York area. The students merely counted the number of black and beige raincoats. My statistics held up at approximately four to one in either case, and I could now say that in the New York area, the upper-middle class generally wore beige raincoats and the lower-middle class generally wore black ones.

My next step was to take a rainy-day count in the two different socioeconomic areas in Chicago, Los Angeles, Dallas, Atlanta and six equally widespread small towns. The research again held up; statistics came back from the cities at about four to one and from the small towns at about two-and-a-half to three to one. (The statistics were not quite that clear cut, but averaged out into those ranges.)

From these statistics I was able to state that in the United States, the beige raincoat is generally worn by members of the upper-middle class and the black raincoat generally worn by members of the lower-middle class. From this, I was able to hypothesize that since these raincoats were an intrinsic part of the American environment, they had in all probability conditioned people by their predominance in certain classes, and automatic (Pavlovian) reactions could be expected.

In short, when someone met a man in a beige raincoat, he was likely to think of him as a member of the upper-middle class, and when he met a man in a black raincoat, he was likely to think of him as a member of the lower-middle class. I then had to see if my hypothesis would hold up under testing.

My first test was conducted with 1362 people—a cross section of the general public. They were given an "extrasensory perception" test in which they were asked to guess the answers to a number of problems to which the solutions (they were told) could only be known through ESP. The percentage of correct answers would indicate their ESP quotient. Naturally, a participant in this type of test attempts to get the right answer every time and has no reason to lie, since he wants to score high.

In this test, among a group of other problems and questions, I inserted a set of almost identical "twin pictures." There was only one variable. The twin pictures showed the same man in the same pose dressed in the same suit, the same shirt, the same tie, the same shoes. The only difference was the raincoat—one black, one beige. Participants were told that the pictures were of twin brothers, and were asked to identify the most prestigious of the two. Over 87 percent, or 1118 people, chose the man in the beige raincoat.

I next ran a field test. Two friends and I wore beige raincoats for one month, then switched to black raincoats the following month. We attempted to duplicate our other clothing during both months. At the end of each month, we recorded the general attitude of people toward us—waiters, store clerks, business associates, etc. All three of us agreed that the beige raincoat created a distinctly better impression upon the people we met.

Finally, I conducted one additional experiment alone. Picking a group of business offices at random, I went into each office with a *Wall Street Journal* in a manila envelope and asked the receptionist or secretary to allow me to deliver it personally it to the man in charge. When wearing a black raincoat, it took me a day and a half to deliver twenty-five papers. In a beige raincoat, I was able to deliver the same number in a single morning.

The impression transmitted to receptionists and secretaries by my black raincoat and a nondescript suit, shirt and tie clearly was that I was a glorified delivery boy, and so I had to wait or was never admitted. But their opinion of me was substantially altered by the beige raincoat worn with the same other clothes. They thought I might be an associate or friend of the boss because that is what I implied, and they had better let me in. In short, they reacted to years of preconditioning and accepted the beige raincoat as a symbol of authority and status while they rejected the black raincoat as such.

This study was conducted in 1971. And although more and more lower-middle class men are wearing beige raincoats each year (basically because of improved wash-and-wear methods that make them much less expensive to keep clean), the results of the study remain valid and will continue to be for years to come. You cannot wear a black raincoat, and you must wear a beige raincoat—if you wish to be accepted as a member of the upper-middle class and treated accordingly (among all other raincoat colors, only dark blue tests as acceptable).

I continue to test the beige raincoat each year in my multiple-item studies. In the field of clothing, multiple-item studies are those that incorporate an entire look: the upper-middle-class look, the lower-middle-class look, etc. These studies usually are not geared to test people's responses to specific items, but if a particular item is not consistent with the rest, it will destroy the effectiveness of the study because the incongruous item spoils the total look.

In one multiple-item study, I sent a twenty-five-year-old male college graduate from an upper-middle-class midwestern background to 100 offices. To fifty of them he wore an outfit made up entirely of garments that had been previously tested as having lower-middle-class characteristics; to the remaining fifty he wore an outfit of garments that had been previously tested as having upper-middle-class characteristics. Prior to his arrival at each office, I had arranged for the man in charge to tell his secretary that he had hired an assistant, and to instruct her to show the young man around. The executive also made sure that his secretary would not be going to lunch, would not be going home, and would not be overworked at the time of my man's arrival.

After being shown through the offices, which took anywhere from fifteen minutes to an hour, depending on the secretary and the office, the young man made a series of requests. He first asked for something simple like letterhead stationery or a pencil and pad. The responses of the secretaries to these requests had no statistical significance, although the young man did note that there was a substantial difference in attitude. In upper-middle-class garb, he received the requested item with no comment, but perjorative comments or quizzical looks were directed toward him at least one-third of the time when he wore lower-middle-class clothing.

Once the first request sequence was completed, the young man gave each secretary a standardized order. Before going to each office, he had been given the names of three people in the files of the office. These names were written on a card, and his procedure was always the same. Putting the card on the secretary's desk, he would say, "Miss (always using her name) Jones, please get these files for me; I will be at Mr. Smith's desk." He would then walk away, trying not to give the secretary a chance to answer him verbally. The results were quite significant.

In upper-middle-class garb, he received the files within ten minutes forty-two times. In lower-middle-class garb, he received the files only twelve times. Perjorative comments were directed at him twelve times while wearing upper-middle-class clothes, and eight times while wearing lower-middle-class clothes. This means that he received positive responses only four times out of fifty while wearing lower-middle-class garb; but he received positive responses thirty times out of fifty when he was wearing upper-middle-class garb.

From this experiment and many others like it, I was able to conclude that in upper-middle-class clothes, a young man will be more successful in giving orders to secretaries.

The experiment will give you an idea of why I have spent

so many years and so much of my clients' money in determining what constitutes upper-middle-class dress. It is obvious from the experiment that secretaries, who generally were not members of the upper-middle class, did in fact recognize upper-middle-class clothing, if not consciously then at least subconsciously, and they did react to it. The reactions of the secretaries indicate that dress is neither trivial nor frivolous, but an essential element in helping a man to function in the business world with maximum effectiveness.

But does everyone react as the secretaries did?

For years, some companies have been attempting to increase the efficiency of employees by prescribing dress and establishing dress codes. Most of these schemes have proved ineffective because they have been created by amateurs who don't understand the effect clothing has on the work environment. Dress codes *can* work, as I will show later, but the assumption that clothing has a major, continuing impact on the wearer is erroneous. True, you may feel shabby when you wear shabby clothes, and your morale may perk up a bit when you splurge on an expensive tie. But clothing most significantly affects the people whom the wearer meets and, in the long run, affects the wearer only indirectly because it controls the reaction of the world to him. My research shows that in most business situations the wearer is not directly affected by his clothing, and that the affect of clothing on other people is mainly controlled by the socioeconomic level of the clothing.

Let me say it straight out: We all wear uniforms and our uniforms are clear and distinct signs of class. We react to them accordingly. In almost any situation where two men meet, one man's clothing is saying to the other man: "I am more important than you are, please show respect"; or "I am your equal and expect to be treated as such"; or "I am not your equal and I do not expect to be treated as such."

A Twentieth-Century Approach to Clothing

THE "PUSH TEST"

I tested this hypothesis by using what I call the "push test." I took two men, both in their thirties, both of average height and weight, and dressed one in lower-middle-class clothes, the other in upper-middle-class apparel. On the second day of testing, we reversed the clothes so that the men's personalities and physical characteristics would not interfere with the results. We then went into the street and created minor conflict situations.

First, the man in upper-middle-class dress stood to the side of a revolving door at the entrance to a building. When he saw someone coming, he attempted to pace his steps so that he and the approaching party would reach the door at exactly the same time. At that point, we would see which man stepped aside.

In fifty-eight out of eighty-six attempts, our man went through first without any confrontation whatsoever; the other party simply stepped aside. In twelve confrontations the other man looked at him and seemed to say, "Look, buddy, who do you think you are?" but eventually let him through. In the rest of the attempts, the other individual walked through first, indicating by his actions that he was more important.

When the same test was conducted sixty-two times with our man in lower-middle-class clothes, he was pushed aside more often, and on three separate occasions he was threatened with physical violence, each time by other men wearing lower-middle-class garb.

The next day, when we reversed the clothing, the statistics held up: The man in upper-middle-class garb was allowed to pass through the door first on an average of three to one times. The man in the lower-middle-class uniform was threatened with physical violence on two occasions. We became afraid that he would be punched in the nose if we continued, so we stopped the test after twenty runs.

In another test, I again gave two men lower- and upper-middle-class clothing, and had them alternate the looks every other day. Their procedure was to go into stores, of all types and socioeconomic levels, and select some merchandise. When it came time to pay, they would search their pockets, say that they had left their wallets at home, and ask to pay by check.

Too many variables run through a test such as this to put any weight on a small statistical difference. But in both these cases the differences were enormous: My men were able to cash *twice* as many checks wearing upper-middle-class clothing as they did wearing lower-middle-class garb. This means that in many cases the store made the decision to pass up a sale rather than trust a man wearing clothing that looked cheap. Believe me: If you dress like a man of substance and integrity, you will, more often than not, be treated as such.

One of the most significant studies I ever did, from a business point of view, utilized volunteer executives from a company I had worked for with offices in New York, Chicago, Kansas City and on the West Coast. Each man (two from each office) went to two executive headhunter outfits in his city, applying for a specific position, and handling the interview as best he could. For his trip to the first headhunter, the volunteer wore a strict, correct combination of conservative upper-middle-class clothing. When he went to the second headhunter, applying for a similar job, he wore a basic combination of upper-middle-class clothing, but broke one rule: either wearing a lower-middle-class patterned tie; or a shirt that was a bit too bright; or a suit that wasn't as good as it should have been. One man dressed in his most expensive, classiest outfit, but wore his son's cowboy boots.

If anything, the men had a verbal advantage for their second interviews because they had just been through the same drill earlier in the day and knew the ropes. Yet in seven out of the eight cases, the executives reported that the interview had gone much better when they wore their unflawed wardrobe.

Four of the eight men actually received offers from four of the headhunters to arrange interviews with prospective employers. In *each* of those four cases, the offer was made by a headhunter who had interviewed a man wearing perfect upper-middle-class combinations. None of the headhunters who had interviewed the men in their flawed combinations made any offer.

Most large industries are involved in the same major endeavor—making money—and anything that increases efficiency helps them to make more. Many of my client-sponsored studies have been directed accordingly. Several years ago, one large corporation hired me to conduct such a study in two of its branch offices. In one office, a dress code was being enforced for all men in positions of authority—that is, men who had direct responsibility for someone under them. In the second office, there was no dress code, and a rather lax attitude of dress was typical of most of the executives.

First, I tested the relative efficiency of the offices. A time study yielded the following results: The secretaries and clerks in the non-dress-code office spent 4 percent less time at their desks, 5 percent less time actually at their typewriters or equivalent work, and they were absent or late 3 to 5 percent more often than the workers in the office where the dress code was enforced.

I then established a dress code for the non-dress-code office, and it was enforced for one year. The code was an unwritten one, never formally declared, but the word was passed down from above, and it took about six months for everyone to realize it was there. Once they did, most people adhered to it rather strictly. As an adjunct to the dress code, I was brought in on three separate informal occasions to lecture the executives on those colors, patterns and combinations that would help to make them most authoritative and most effective.

At the end of the year, I repeated the time study. In the first office, the performance level was virtually the same as it had been at the beginning of the year. In the second office, where the new dress code had gone into effect, a vast improvement had taken place. The workers now outperformed themselves in every activity that I surveyed. They stayed at their desks 1 percent longer; they worked 2 percent longer; and their lateness and absenteeism were 15 percent improved over the first test.

In addition, the top executives, reporting independently, said that middle-management people were performing at a much better level than they had in the past. And the middle-management people, with one exception, reported that the people working directly under them were performing at a better level than they had in the past.

The significance of this study is not based on the erroneous assumption that clothing changes a man. It is based on the fact that a man's environment changes him, and the clothing worn by people around him is part of his environment. The man who claims he could work as well in his underwear as he could in a $300 suit is probably telling the truth. It's just that if everyone came to work in his underwear, the office wouldn't function as well as if everyone arrived in $300 suits.

HOW TO COMPETE WITH IBM

One of the most intriguing clothing problems I've ever faced was handed to me by a company that competes with IBM in the computer field. Almost everyone in business knows that IBM— at one time officially and now unofficially—enforces a rather strict dress code, particularly for its salesmen, and one of the mandatory staples of this code is the standard white dress shirt. I was supposed to find out:

Is that white dress shirt important?

Does it have anything to do with IBM's spectacular success over competitors?

And if it does, how do you compete with it effectively?

I started out by questioning 106 executives, mostly from the company that had hired me, but also from other IBM competitors in related fields. This was important since some initial research had shown that the backgrounds of the IBM executives, their competitors, and the people who bought from them were almost identical. Generally, they were technically educated, holding bachelor degrees or better, and very conservative in their dress patterns.

With people of this type, it is most unwise to use any direct questioning method; they grasp what you are seeking much too quickly, and then they tend to tell you what they think you want to hear. So I buried my white shirt question in a twin test, using one set of pictures showing men in white shirts and another set of pictures with men wearing other shirts.

Instead of asking questions that would assign socioeconomic values to the shirts, I asked questions that would call for moral values. For instance: Which men would be late to work more often?

Which men would be likely to overstay their lunch hour?

Which men were likely to cheat on their expense account?

Which men were better family men?

Because these were all men whose educational orientations told them to think analytically rather than subjectively, I was somewhat surprised that 87 of the 106 executives attributed greater moral strengths to the white shirt than to the other shirts.

I then questioned the executives directly:

Did they think that a white shirt was an asset to IBM salesmen? Ninety-two said yes.

Did they think that they or their salesmen should wear white shirts in competing with IBM? Eighty-six said yes.

After showing the men the results of my initial survey, 100 agreed that they should adopt the white shirt if they were to compete successfully.

Right?

Wrong!

I next conducted in-depth interviews with fifty-six executives who had in the previous twelve months made major purchases of IBM equipment and consequently had not made major purchases of my client's equipment. The purpose of the interviews was to determine their motivation for making that particular purchase. In all the interviews, the findings were approximately the same. The primary motivation for choosing IBM was a belief in IBM's moral—yes, moral—superiority. In fact, many of the men questioned used the same moral characteristics to describe IBM that were previously attributed to wearers of the white shirt in my twin test.

The men went further, however, and here was the real problem. While forty-six of them attributed moral positives to the wearing of white shirts by IBM salesmen, forty-two of them attributed negative characteristics to any of IBM's competitors wearing white shirts. They considered this an attempt to copy IBM.

All of this is not to say that white shirts were all that the buyers of IBM equipment mentioned. The word that cropped up most frequently was "service," a legitimate area of concern with computer equipment. However, the contracts in most cases were large enough to warrant having special service agreements written in, and my client had on many occasions offered to make special service arrangements with purchasers, who summarily ignored the offer.

I asked forty-two buyers of IBM equipment if they had as much technical knowledge about the products as the people who were selling the equipment to them. Thirty-six said no, so they were making other than a technical decision. And since the IBM equipment was at least as expensive (if not more so) as the equipment of the competition, the men were not making purely economic decisions.

Therefore, although each of the executives was able to cite complicated reasons for their purchases, the white shirt response was glaring in its importance, and I believed that the decision to buy IBM equipment over my client's was largely emotional—based on the positive moral characteristics attributed to the dress of IBM's salesmen.

An allied study that I had conducted on dress as it is used for photographs in advertising had shown that if you put a man next to a computer, the general public would associate the value of the machine with the value attributed to the man's appearance.

So my client still had to combat the superiority of the white shirt; and he was damned if he wore it, and damned if he didn't. After much additional testing, I finally came up with a look composed of a conservative pinstripe suit, a very crisp, narrow pinstriped shirt and a traditionally patterned tie. The look said: "conservative," "reliable," "efficient," "morally upright." It did not say, "copy."

HOW 100 TOP EXECUTIVES DESCRIBED SUCCESSFUL DRESS

Over the years I have conducted literally thousands of studies, experiments and tests to aid my corporate and individual clients in using clothing better and as an indispensable tool of business life. Immediately prior to beginning this book, and specifically for this book, I asked several series of questions of 100 top executives in either medium-sized or major American corporations. The first series was to establish the most up-to-date attitudes on corporate dress.

I showed the executives five pictures of men, each of them wearing expensive, well-tailored, but high-fashion clothing. I asked if this was a proper look for the junior business executive. Ninety-two of the men said no, eight said yes.

I showed them five pictures of men neatly dressed in obvious lower-middle-class attire and asked if these men were dressed in proper attire for a young executive. Forty-six said yes, fifty-four said no.

I next showed them five pictures of men dressed in conservative upper-middle-class clothing and asked if they were dressed in proper attire for the young executive. All one hundred said yes.

I asked them whether they thought the men in the upper-middle-class garb would succeed better in corporate life than the men in the lower-middle-class uniform. Eighty-eight said yes, twelve said no.

I asked if they would choose one of the men in the lower-middle-class dress as their assistant. Ninety-two said no, eight said yes.

I next showed them pictures of four young men. The first had a very short haircut; the second had a moderate haircut with moderate sideburns; the third had a moderate haircut, but with fairly long sideburns; and the fourth had very long hair. I asked which haircut was the most profitable for a young man to wear. Eighty-two of them picked the moderate haircut with moderate sideburns; three picked the very short cut; and fifteen picked the moderate cut with long sideburns. No one picked the long hair.

I next asked if they would hire the man with long hair. Seventy-four said no.

To 100 other top executives of major corporations, I submitted the following written questions:

1. Does your company have a written or an unwritten dress code? Ninety-seven said yes. Three said no. Only two had a written dress code.

2. Would a number of men at your firm have a much better chance of getting ahead if they knew how to dress? Ninety-six said yes, four said no.

3. If there were a course in how to dress for business, would you send your son? All 100 said yes.

4. Do you think employee dress affects the general tone of the office? All 100 said yes.

5. Do you think employee dress affects efficiency? Fifty-two said yes, forty-eight said no.

6. Would you hold up the promotion of a man who didn't dress properly? Seventy-two said yes, twenty-eight said no.

7. Would you tell a young man if his dress was holding him back? Eighty said no, twenty said yes.

8. Does your company at present turn down people who show up at job interviews improperly dressed on that basis alone? Eighty-four said yes, sixteen said no.

9. Would you take a young man who didn't know how to dress as your assistant? Ninety-two said no, eight said yes.

10. Do you think there is a need for a book that would

explain to a young man how to dress? Ninety-four said yes, six said no.

11. Do you think there is a need for a book to tell people in business how to dress? One hundred said yes.

Keep reading, fellows, you got it.

2.

HOW TO GET THE MOST
OUT OF INVESTING
IN SUITS

The suit is the single most important garment that every man wears—and not only because it is the most expensive and requires the greatest amount of time for selection and fitting. It is the garment on which most people judge the wearer's status, character and abilities. And because it covers the upper torso, which is the focal point of most people with whom we communicate, it is the central power garment—the garment that establishes our position as inferior, equal, or superior in any in-person business situation.

Suits are positive authority symbols, worn by the upper middle class—the people who make important decisions in our lives. We are much more likely to believe, respect and obey the man who wears a suit than the man who does not. Men who do not wear suits may have important functions in our society, but we do not normally accord them such in our minds. In any level of society, suits are associated with authority, with position, with power.

Because of their importance and because no item of clothing can be dealt with in isolation, suits will be the subject of commentary throughout this book. This chapter merely establishes the basics.

HOW TO BUY A SUIT

Most men believe that a suit is bought in a fifteen-minute period when they go into a store, walk to a rack, select a suit, have it fitted and leave. They not only believe this; it's how they do it, and it's wrong.

If you have only fifteen minutes to buy a suit on a given day, don't buy one that day. If you are going to buy a suit, plan that purchase in advance. Decide what you need: color, pattern, texture, weight, material and style. Know your approximate size. And decide how much, within a certain range, you are willing to spend. For any businessman, buying a suit should be a serious, thoughtful endeavor, not a casual splurge.

When you go to buy a suit, wear the best-looking and best-fitting suit you already own. If you are going to buy a suit with a vest, wear a vest. Wear a dress shirt of the weight and style you believe you will be wearing with the new suit. It also helps if the shirt you are wearing is of a color that will be compatible with the color of the suit you hope to buy. Wear a good tie of a color and pattern that will not clash tremendously with the color and pattern of the suit you hope to buy.

If you are going to buy a suit that has belted pants (as business suits should), wear a belt. Carry with you all items that you normally carry in your suit pockets. Wear the type of shoes that you expect to wear with the new suit.

On any Saturday, in any upper-middle-class store, you can see otherwise astute, affluent businessmen buying suits. The only problem is that they have come dressed in jeans or sport slacks, heavy wool shirts or sweaters, and Hush Puppies, boots or sneakers. That any of these customers are able to buy suits that are appropriate and well-fitting when such attire is a miracle, with which most of them are not blessed.

There is a more important reason for being properly dressed

when buying a suit, and in this case the female shopping-instinct serves far better than the male. Any woman will tell you that when she goes clothes shopping, she goes dressed to the gills. She does so because she knows that clothing store clerks will judge her and treat her according to the clothes she is wearing, and she wants and expects to be treated bloody well. Men should do the same, for exactly the same reason.

Once in the store, properly dressed, you will sooner or later be greeted by a clerk. Let him know immediately that *you*, not he, are in the authority position and that you know exactly what you are doing. You do this by describing, as specifically as you can, the type of suit for which you are looking and your size. If you do this, the clerk will not try to push everything in the store on you; unless he is spectacularly inept, he knows that men who know what they are doing become annoyed by such tactics. If he does try to push anything on you, do become annoyed, and show it.

Let the clerk lead you to the suits and show you where your size is kept. Then ask him to let you look through the stack on your own. Some sales people will and some won't. If he insists on staying, let him—he may even turn out to be helpful—but do not let him distract you or pressure you. If you see no suits that meet your basic requirements, leave—immediately. Do not decide to settle for anything until you have exhausted every outlet within reasonable reach.

If you do find a suit, or suits, that meet your basic requirements, begin to look at it very carefully. Feel the material, and know what it is. Read the label if you must. Look at the stitching behind the collar to see that it is neat, even and reinforced. Examine the lining, keeping in mind that it must be sewn securely enough to stand up to dry cleaning. With most winter and all-weather clothes, it is preferable if they are fully lined. Check for required interior pockets. Look at the workmanship of the buttonholes to make sure that the stitching will hold up for several years of wear; look at the buttons. Are they cheap plastic or expensive bone? Are they sewn on securely?

How to Get the Most Out of Investing in Suits

If the suit has any pattern, regardless of what that pattern is, look carefully at every place where material is sewn. There is little that looks worse in a suit than a pattern that is improperly joined. It is an immediate tipoff to poor workmanship or an attempt to save material—neither of which you are going to pay for, I hope.

If all the above aspects and any others that are of concern to you are satisfactory, then you are ready for your final test. Grasp the sleeve of the suit jacket in both hands and twist it tightly for a few seconds. The clerk will probably have a heart attack, but this test must be done. If the sleeve immediately springs back to shape, it's a wearable suit. If wrinkles remain ... well, you've just wrinkled a suit you're not going to buy. The suit will wrinkle the minute you sit down; you'll look like a bum most of the time; and your pressing bills will be enormous. Don't buy it.

EVERYTHING YOU NEVER KNEW ABOUT GETTING A SUIT FITTED

When you have tentatively settled on a suit, you now come to the big hurdle—the fitting. As the clerk is leading you to the fitting room, tell him in affable but firm language that you wish to be fitted by the head fitter, or, if possible, by the tailor who is actually going to do the work on the suit. Some clerks will be upset and antagonized by this, but if you are dressed as you should be, and if you have followed all my previous advice, by this time he should be attuned to the fact that you are important and accustomed to getting your way without compromise.

When the tailor or fitter arrives, take him aside, tell him you're very particular about your suits and ask him to give it some extra effort. Then slip him a few dollars. This introduces a new element into men's clothes buying: tipping the tailor. Virtually no one does it; the tailor will be grateful because everyone likes money; you will get extra effort; and that is what you need because it pays off. I'll leave the amount up to you, depending on the quality of the store and the cost of the suit, but generally I would suggest no less than $5.00 and no more than $10.00.

You are now ready to try on the pants—and only the pants. When doing so, put on your belt and put in your pockets all those items that you normally carry in your suit pants. You should also wear your shoes, because pants cannot be measured properly without shoes.

Pants are always fitted from the top down, and the first area of fit you must check is the waist. The proper position for a man's pants waist is slightly above the navel, and exactly horizontal to the ground, all the way around. They should not be lower in the front than in the back. Fitters will often tell you to adjust your pants to the height you normally wear them. If you wear them wrong, then it's high time for you to change your habits—and for the best of reasons. There is a very definite tendency on the part of lower-middle-class men to let their pants droop and hang from the hips. Upper-middle-class men wear them correctly.

For some men—because they are either tall and thin or short and heavy—some suit pants will have waists that are either too high or too low, because all rack suits are made proportionate to the average man wearing that size. If the waist is too high or too low and cannot be corrected, take off the pants and do not buy the suit. You do not want to look like Lou Costello with his pants under his armpits, and you do not want to look like a member of the lower-middle class.

Assuming that the height of the waist is correct, then it should neither be too loose nor too tight. It is too loose if it does not fit smoothly all the way around, and if material bulges under the belt. It is too loose if it slips at all when you move. It is too tight if you cannot comfortably slip the flat of your hand in and out.

Moving down, the next area that must be fitted is the seat area. If your waist is proportionately larger than your seat area, frequently the pants will sag and be baggy; if your seat area is proportionately larger than your waist, the pants may be too tight. In either case, the problem should be corrected so that the seat area is smooth but comfortable when standing and sitting. If the seat area is too large, have the fitter *pin it* rather than chalk it. When material is taken from the seat area, this very definitely effects the way the bottoms of the pants hang, and the measurement that must be taken for the cuffs. This is also true of the crotch, which should also not be baggy or tight. If the crotch is too big, have that area pinned also, if possible, or at least have it held so that the cuffs may be measured accurately.

The final aspect of pants fit is the length. The decision of whether to finish the bottoms with turned up cuffs or with plain bottoms is yours. If you prefer plain bottoms, they should break in front and be one-half to three-quarters of an inch longer in the back. If you wear cuffs, it is usually best if they are tailored so they hang exactly horizontal to the ground and there are no wrinkles or bulges when the cuff fold is made. (See drawing on pg. 74).

Whenever I have a suit fitted, I always ask that the cuffs be made as long as possible without drooping or dragging the floor. I ask this explicitly because, despite all assurances to the contrary, almost all suit materials shrink after a few cleanings. Knits stretch somewhat in the beginning, but they begin to shrink later. And it is much less troublesome to have pants shortened than to have them lengthened.

If the pants fit you properly in the waist, seat and crotch and do not require pinning, you are ready to move on to the rest of the suit while you're still wearing the pants. If they do not fit you in the waist, seat or crotch and must be corrected, put back on the pants you wore into the store before you try on the rest of the suit.

If the suit has a vest, it must also be fitted—and pinned. Because of its appropriate closeness to the body, it is particularly important when fitting a vest that the shirt you have on under it is of the weight that you will be wearing underneath the suit. A vest should fit smoothly, with no pulling or sagging when sitting or standing. The armholes should be open enough for comfort but not sag. The back should have no wrinkles and not ride up during normal activity. Keep it on and move around in it until you're sure it's right. If it is not pinned, keep it on when trying on the jacket. If it is pinned, put on the vest you brought with you. If you are buying a suit with a vest, always have the jacket fitted with a vest on underneath it.

When you put on any suit jacket, the first and most important aspect is how it feels. I don't care how it looks, if it does not feel perfectly comfortable sitting, standing and moving around, then don't buy it. You're going to have to wear it a long time, and you may as well not start out wrong.

It is very difficult to describe exactly how a suit jacket should fit. But a perfectly fitting suit is very easy to spot, and if you want to see someone whose suits always fit perfectly, watch Johnny Carson. His colors and patterns are sometimes inappropriate for the average businessman, but they are always impeccably fitted. They do not wrinkle or bulge; they do not gap or pull. If you can come even close to this look, then you're going to look good.

As with the pants, the fit of the jacket begins at the top, at the neck. Look at the neck area carefully; if it does not fit absolutely flat, with no wrinkles or bulges, tell the fitter to fix it. Now there's something about this area you must know. When a custom-tailored suit is being made, the body of the jacket is made and fitted before the collar is attached. When that is perfect, the collar is fitted and attached.

On rack suits, to repair major problems in this area, the collar must be fully or partially removed, and tailors hate to do this, since it is meticulous, time-consuming work. Consequently, many of them simply take in a tuck, and a great number of men —at least half of those reading this book—end up walking around with a bubble, or what I call a miniature knapsack on their backs.

If there's a problem in this area, tell the tailor you want it done right. If he knows that you know he will probably do it right the first time, because if he doesn't he'll get it back. Many men have this problem because they do not have perfect posture, and the sizes and proportions of rack suits are manufactured for the man with perfect posture.

The jacket must next fit around the chest and waist. While being fitted for the jacket, you will hopefully not have forgotten to put into the interior pockets those items—wallet, cigarettes, etc.—that you normally carry there. If the fitter asks you to remove them, as many will, tell him no, because that's the way you will be wearing it, and that's the way you expect it to fit. If he says it can't be done, buy your suits elsewhere. The chest should fit smoothly all the way around, with no wrinkles or bulges and no gapping or sagging of the lapels.

If you have a thin waist, your jacket should be a bit more tightly fitted than if you are heavy. The reason is that when you sit, the jacket will tend to bulge if you have a bit of a stomach; but it won't if you don't. The best way to judge this is after the tailor has pinned it. Sit down with the jacket buttoned and see how it looks. If it pulls noticeably, have it adjusted.

The standard method used to determine if a jacket is the proper length is to stand straight with your arms straight down your sides, your hands flat against the sides of the jacket. Now curl your fingers under the bottom of the jacket. If the bottom just fits into the curl, it is correct. If it is visibly longer or shorter, don't buy that suit; it can't be corrected. Naturally, if your arms are much shorter or longer than usual for a man of your size, make sure that the tailor takes this into account and makes the proper adjustments.

The tip of the jacket sleeves should come approximately five inches off the tip of the thumb, never more than five and one-half. If they are any higher, you will end up looking like a Broadway crapshooter, a fashion model or some other dandy of no substance. If you intend to wear French cuffs with the suit, you should wear same to the fitting. Today, some suits will not accommodate French cuffs because the suit sleeves are too tight, and this is a severe limitation you should keep in mind.

Once you and the fitter have done the best you can with the

suit, stand back and look at it. Walk around; sit down—but watch those pins. If you decide to take it, give it to the fitter, making sure to tell him to save for you the material taken from the cuffs of the pants—for reasons I will tell you later.

Arrange for the date when the suit will allegedly be picked up. I say allegedly because, nine times out of ten, the suit is going to need more work to make it just right. If you must wear the suit on the fifteenth, do not agree to pick it up on the fourteenth. Try to pick it up on the sixth.

NOW FOR THE SECOND FITTING

When you return, allow yourself enough time—take enough time—to see that it fits absolutely correctly. The man who wears tailor-made suits goes in for numerous time-consuming fittings. He knows how important it is or he wouldn't have or be spending that kind of money. The difference between a good fit and a bad fit is very often the second fitting, and too many men simply ignore this point. Don't. Insist on it even if it causes long faces and the suit is carefully wrapped up and ready to go. (see drawing on page 39)

When you go back, the procedure is exactly as before: pants first, vest next, then the entire suit. Stand in the five-way mirror, and look at each item and the entire suit from every angle. If there is anything, no matter how minor, that you do not like, tell the tailor you want it fixed. If he says it can't be done, demand your money back and leave him the suit; if they sold it to you in the first place, then it can be fixed. You're paying for a suit that fits—so get it.

Two types of men go into restaurants and clothing stores. Some men they throw things at; other men they serve. The difference between the two is that the latter *insists* on service.

If, for any reason, you must take the suit to wear for a special occasion even though there are still problems that require adjustment, take it only with the understanding that it can be fixed later.

The Right Suit (Left) and the Wrong Suit (Right)

About a month or a month and a half after you have bought a suit and worn it and had it cleaned, put it on and look at it again carefully. If it has shrunk or stretched or sagged or bagged, back it goes to the store for another adjustment. Most materials do have some change in fit after a time, and if this change is noticeable, it is your right and your duty as an aware consumer to take it back and have it fixed. If the store will not accommodate you, then you should no longer buy there.

One of the most important characteristics of a good upper-middle-class suit is that it fits you and you alone—not everyone like you. It is specifically tailored for the man who must wear it. If your size corresponds perfectly to a suit manufacturer's rendering of that size, you can buy your suits almost anywhere, since fitting only requires minor, standard adjustments. If you have problems with your size, if every rack suit you buy has to have major plastic surgery before it hangs right, then you will be much better off if you buy your suits only in the more expensive stores.

The reason is, quite simply, that better stores have better fitters and tailors than less expensive stores. In the less expensive stores, only minor tailoring services are offered at no extra charge, and even if you paid for more work it probably wouldn't be of the best. Better stores never charge extra for tailoring, and although you may have to pay from $25 to $50 more for a suit, you are getting much more than that in quality and fit. A suit that doesn't fit is wasted money, no matter how great a bargain it seems to be.

HOW TO BUY SEMI-CUSTOM SUITS

The preceding advice is for the man who buys mass-manufactured, off-the-rack suits, which includes about 99 percent of us. Of the two other kinds of suit, the full- and semi-custom, I will not touch on the full-custom here; it generally runs from $500 to $600,* and is available to very few men.

*All prices in this book are based on mid-1975 levels.

When you can afford that kind of money to buy that kind of suit, you don't need much advice anyway.

Semi-custom suits are just that and are sold in many stores, including better department stores. They range in price from approximately $275 to $450, which makes them about $150 more expensive than an off-the-rack suit of similar quality. What semi-customs offer is fit, particularly for those men who have great difficulty in that area with off-the-rack suits.

Basically, the buyer of semi-custom suiting is shown swatches from which he chooses color and pattern; he is offered a wide variety of styling and detail; and a number of measurements are taken. His suit is then run up in small shops, either on or off the premises. Several fittings are required.

There are certain things the buyer of semi-custom suits should demand: that the measurements be taken by the head tailor; that the suit have all necessary interior pockets; and that the suit be fully lined. He should also insist that the suit have functional button-cuffs, that they actually button and unbutton. Stores will resist this, and give any number of excuses not to do it. The favorite copout is that once functional buttons are added, the sleeves can no longer be shortened or lengthened and since the suit is being made elsewhere this is impossible unless you are willing to gamble up to $450 that the sleeves will fit correctly the first time. Your answer to this is that the suit can originally be made without functional button cuffs and these can be added locally (at their expense of course) after the last fitting.

Since functional button-cuffs are the most immediately noticeable attribute of a custom suit, anyone with any brains at all insists on them. After all, why pay for a semi-custom suit that is no better than a suit off the rack? Semi-customs are wonderful, but they should look as if they're wonderful.

HOW TO CHOOSE MATERIALS

The best material a suit can be made from is wool. Wool takes dyes better than any other fabric. It doesn't snag; it fits well; it doesn't lose its shape; it is resilient; it lays better on the body; in winter it's warmer; and it outlasts any other fabric. It can also be woven into many different textures and looks.

The second best suit fabric is the polyester and wool blend. Although this is primarily found in lighter weight suits, it has all the attributes of wool and is slightly less expensive.

Texturized polyester suits can be very good or very bad, depending on the material. The only safe yardstick for the non-expert is price. Texturized polyester can look very rich, can look like wool and be tailored very neatly. If a polyester suit does have the look of wool, if you can't tell the difference without being told, buy it. If it does not, then don't buy it. Texturized polyester wrinkles almost not at all, and holds its creases and shape remarkably well.

Because it is so good, texturized polyester is replacing the knit in all but the cheapest outlets—and with good reason. Knit suits are terrible; they snag and bag and stretch and shrink—they do everything you do not want a suit to do. They are also hot, and all but the most expensive are ugly.

Polyester and cotton blends are excellent in lightweight summer suits, but because of their predominantly light colors, light linings and workmanship commensurate with their comparatively inexpensive price, they rarely last beyond one season of hard wear. The lightweight polyester and wool suit is just as comfortable in warm weather; it looks richer to begin with; and in the end it is a better buy because it lasts longer.

Cotton suits and linen suits are extremely comfortable in warm weather, but any pure cotton wrinkles after only several hours and so these suits are just not practical for the man who must consistently look well-groomed.

Suits are made from dozens more materials and blends, but all aspects considered, they are best avoided. Any suit with nylon or rayon in it is likely to be worthless, and suits with any percentage of mohair or silk rarely have an appropriate look for business wear. Corduroy and denim suits are legitimately worn by some men in high-fashion industries—advertising, radio, television—but for most of us they should be regarded as sportswear only.

The fact is that nine out of every ten good business suits are made from wool or wool blends, and most men would do just as well if they never wore anything else.

PICKING COLORS AND PATTERNS

In addition to fit, the most important aspects of suits are color and pattern. The proper colors for a gentleman's suit are blue, gray and beige, and shades thereof. Any man who sticks within those categories and doesn't get into the hybrids (greenish blue or greenish gray) or weird, inappropriate shades like electric blue will always be appropriately dressed. Browns and blacks are sometimes acceptable, but because of the many times when they are not, I would suggest that most men avoid them.

Suit patterns are relatively simple. Solid suits, the staple of every man's wardrobe, should look rich and soft if they are standard business suits. Linen and denim should look rich, but are rarely soft.

Two types of stripe are acceptable in men's business suiting. The first is the pinstripe, and it is a very narrow vertical stripe. The greatest majority of these have white or blue stripes, and although other color stripes are acceptable, white is by far the most sophisticated. The only time a pinstripe will give you trouble is when it is orange, rust or purple. These colors are hell to coordinate with shirts and ties, and thus limit the use of the suit tremendously.

Chalk stripes are wider than pinstripes, generally about an eighth of an inch; and they are very tricky. A chalk-stripe suit can label you a Wall Street executive or a Chicago gangster— and with only the slightest variation (see drawing page 44). If a chalk-stripe suit looks gaudy, don't buy it; if it looks conservative, do, preferably with a vest.

Several types of plaid suits are acceptable (see color drawings page 70). The first is an almost invisible plaid. There's a plaid there, but you must look carefully in order to see it. The suit is usually of a dark color, with the pattern woven in threads

Chalk-Stripe Suits

The Wall Street Businessman Look   The Chicago Gangster Look

of slightly lighter or slightly darker shades of the same color. This suit is always acceptable.

The next plaid is what I call the standard businessman's plaid. It is obviously a plaid, but it is subtle; you have to look carefully to see what colors are in it. This is a traditionally summer suit in lighter colors, but is also found in winter suiting.

The Glen plaid is a discernible plaid, which has both definition and shape to it. With this pattern, you must avoid (as you did with the pinstripe) shades of orange, purple or rust, not because they will make it a less acceptable suit, but because they are so difficult to match with shirts and ties.

In the plaid category, a certain indefinable line separates acceptable business patterns from strictly sportswear patterns. Entire suits of the latter patterns should not be worn by any serious businessman. The only rule I can give is: If you think that the jacket of a plaid suit could possibly be worn separately as a sport jacket, then don't buy it.

Any simple box pattern repeated on a suit has the same effect as the more traditional plaids. Such patterns are perfectly acceptable, if they are simple, with clean lines and of appropriate colors.

The last acceptable pattern in suiting is really a combination of patterns lumped into the same group. I call it the beefy British look. The material is always wool and the patterns run from the traditional herringbone to the tweed and Donegal tweed. They are all basically the same in effect; they are only worn in northern climes, and they are very definitely a symbol of the upper-middle class.

While some other suit patterns might be acceptable for business wear, they are rare, tricky and should be avoided. If any man wishes to be safe, he will stick with the aforementioned. If you must have razzle-dazzle in your clothing, save it for sportswear.

THE PSYCHOLOGICAL ASSOCIATION OF SUITS

Because the suit is the central power garment in any business combination, it is the garment that will most influence any viewer's stereotyped judgment of the wearer. It immediately establishes authority, credibility and likability—those qualities most important in any business interaction.

The darker the suit, the more authority it transmits. A black suit is more authoritative than a dark blue, although it is much too powerful for most men and should be rarely worn anyway because of its funereal overtones. The most authoritative pattern is the pinstripe, followed in descending order by the solid, the chalk stripe and the plaid. If you need to be more authoritative, stick with dark pinstripes. But if you are a very large man or if you already have a great sense of presence or if you have a gruff or swarthy appearance, it is best to trim down your authority so that people will not be frightened by you. This can be accomplished by wearing lighter shades of blue and gray and beiges.

Suits that will give you the most credibility with people of the upper-middle class are dark blue and dark gray solids and pinstripes of both colors. But note: Only the dark blue solid will give you high credibility with the lower-middle class.

If you must be authoritative and credible with both the upper-middle class and the lower-middle class at the same time —say you are a banker or a lawyer and must deal daily with a wide variety of people—light blue and light gray solids accomplish this, although the light blue is generally not considered an acceptable suit for the truly conservative businessman.

The suits in which men are more likely to be liked are again light gray and light blue solids and medium-range business plaids. Bright plaids sometimes turn off the upper-middle class.

The following examples of the most important business suits provide more specific information. If a suit is categorized as "neutral," that means it will neither help nor hurt you, but is not recommended. "Before the public" means speaking before any group of people where television is not present.

SOLID NAVY: The upper-middle class likes it. The lower-middle class likes it and respects you in it. Large men should not wear it. Small men should not wear it. Heavy men should wear it. On thin men it's neutral. Before the public it's fine. On television it's fine. If you're a weak authority figure it's excellent. If you're a strong authority figure it's bad.

SOLID DARK GRAY: This is a positive with the upper-middle class, a negative with the lower middle class. It is excellent for large men and negative for small men. It is good for heavy men, neutral on thin men. Before the public it is excellent, as it is on television. If you're a weak authority figure, use it. If you are a strong authority figure, it is neutral.

DARK BLUE PINSTRIPE: It is positive with the upper-middle class, negative with the lower-middle class. Tall men should not wear it. Short men should wear it. Heavy men should wear it. Thin men should not wear it. No striped suit should ever be worn on television; they look beautiful on the monitor, but if there's reception trouble at home, the pinstripes jump all over the place and reduce concentration or attention. The pinstripe is an excellent suit for addressing the public off television. If you have authority problems, it is the best. If you come on too strong, it's bad.

DARK GRAY PINSTRIPE: The upper-middle class likes it; the lower-middle class does not. On tall and short men it's neutral. On heavy men it's positive, one of the better suits for them. On thin men, it's a negative. It's positive before the public. It's positive for men with authority problems, negative for anyone who comes on too strong.

MEDIUM BLUE SOLID: This is a positive with both classes, a suit that can be worn anywhere. Tall men should wear it and short men should wear it. It is neutral on heavy men, neutral on thin men and neutral before the public. On television, it is excellent. It is good for people with authority problems and with strong authority figures.

MEDIUM GRAY SOLID: This is positive with the upper-middle class, negative with the lower-middle class. On tall men it is excellent. On short men it is neutral. On heavy men it is negative. On thin men it is positive. It is neutral before the public and on television. If you have trouble giving orders it's neutral. If you are a strong authority figure it's a positive, taking the edge off your aggressiveness.

MEDIUM GRAY PINSTRIPE: This is liked by the upper-middle class, disliked by the lower-middle class. It's a negative on tall men, positive on short men. It's neutral on heavy men, thin men and before the public. It's positive on those who find it difficult to give orders, negative on those who come on too strong.

MEDIUM BLUE PINSTRIPE: This is positive with the upper-middle class, negative with the lower-middle class. It is negative on short men, neutral on heavy men, negative on thin men, neutral before the public. It is a good authority-boosting suit and also, surprisingly, positive if you come on strong.

LIGHT BLUE SOLID: This is positive with both classes. It is positive on tall men and thin men, negative on short men and heavy men. It is negative before the public, not bad on television. If you have trouble giving orders, don't wear it. If you're too strong, it's good.

LIGHT GRAY SOLID: It is positive with both classes and on tall men. It is negative on short men, negative on heavy men, positive on thin men. It is negative before the public, positive on television. It is negative for those who have trouble giving orders, positive if you come on strong.

DARK BROWN: This is a negative with the upper-middle class, only neutral with the lower-middle class. It is negative on all men except heavy men. It is negative before the public and on television. It is negative if you are trying to be more authoritative and negative if you are too authoritative. It's one of the worst suits made and should be avoided. It is also an immediate and strong negative with people who are Jewish, particularly those over forty-five, although I do not know the reason for this aversion.

THE SUIT VERSUS THE SPORT JACKET

Sooner or later, most of my clients ask if it is ever appropriate to wear sport jackets to the office. Some indicate that other men in their firm do. The answer is no. In every comparative test I have ever conducted—using such standards as integrity, ability or even "Which man would you want as a friend?"—the suit has won hands down. The only exception is when the effect of an immediately recognizable upper-middle-class sport jacket, such as a camel hair worn with a pair of dark blue slacks, is measured against the effect of an obviously lower-middle-class suit. But otherwise the suit wins in all other comparisons.

PICKING YOUR STYLE

Disregarding color and pattern, all suits have a style, or cut. This cut ranges from the very conservative, traditional Brooks Brothers suit which has changed hardly at all in twenty years to the highly fitted suit turned out by many of the European designers, Pierre Cardin being the most prominent example.

The highly fitted suit does have its place—women love it and it is a staple of men who work in glamour industries—but its place is not in the mainstream of American business. It is not a suit for the office. Any man who wears it in any basic American business will be trusted less, respected less, promoted less, and will sell less while wearing it. Prejudice dies hard, and the men who run America have many prejudices, both conscious and unconscious.

The European designers and the growing fashion consciousness of men *have* had a positive effect on men's styles. Today's typical business suit is much more shaped than it was a few years ago. And within moderation, shaping is fine; it makes men look like people rather than mannequins. But the style of any successful business suit can never be so contoured as to become severe.

Men's styles do change, but they change slowly, and attitudes toward those styles change even more slowly. The best advice I can give any man contemplating any new style is not to buy it the first year it is shown. Wait about a year and a half; if it's still around, in significant quantity and in the better stores, then it may be catching on. Still, I'll be the last person to tell you to run out and buy it even then.

At present, the single-breasted suit is the prevailing style, and it will be for quite some time. Double-breasted suits will come back eventually. When they do, if you are thin, wear them; if you are heavy, do not. Double-breasted suits look terrible on heavy men, regardless of the prevailing style.

Another stylistic element of suits is the vent in the bottom back of the suit jacket. Some suits have center vents and some have side vents. Both are acceptable, but heavy men, particularly those with big behinds, look much better in suits with side vents.

Business suits should be plain: no fancy or extra buttons; no weird color stitching; no flaps on the breast pocket; no patches on the sleeves; no belts in the back of the jacket; no leather ornamentation; no cowboy yokes. Never.

Remember the swatch of material from your new suit that you asked the tailor to save? You're going to need it—when you begin buying your shirts and ties and putting them together. Coming right up.

3.

HOW TO MAXIMIZE
THE POWER OF SHIRTS

In the Middle Ages, when a sovereign committed a crime that put him at loggerheads with the greatest power of the time—the church—he would often expiate himself by putting on a hair shirt and prostrating himself before a cathedral. To all the other potentates in the area, he thereby signaled one of two developments: either he was working himself back into good graces, or his property was up for grabs. The shirt that you wear in the twentieth century can be just as significant a signal to everyone around you. It can either say that you're in good graces—or that your job, your power and your future are up for grabs.

CHOOSING MATERIALS

The most common and most acceptable material from which shirts are made is cotton. The advantages of a cotton shirt are substantial: it feels good to wear; it's soft and smooth; it looks very rich; and it breathes, making it comparatively cool in the summer and in stuffy office buildings. Unfortunately, cotton wrinkles like hell when you're wearing it. And if you must use a commercial laundry, you are undoubtedly well aware of how difficult it is to have a cotton shirt ironed well enough so that at least you don't start the day looking as if you slept in it. Nonetheless, a good-quality, well-tailored cotton shirt offers *the* look you should try to achieve.

The next most popular materials for shirts are the polyester and cotton blends (usually 65 percent polyester and 35 percent cotton, although there are variations). Polyester and cotton shirts are those usually referred to as "wash-and-wear," and while they cannot simply be washed and put on with no ironing at all, they do require only a minimum amount, just a touch-up, to look fine.

The polyester and cottons wrinkle hardly at all, and after long hours of wear look better than cotton. For most men who cannot change their shirts during the work day and still want to look consistently neat, they are almost the perfect shirt. They do, however, tend to retain heat, and usually are not as cool and comfortable as cotton in summer.

A growing number of dress shirts are knits, in many varieties. The only real advantage of a knit shirt is, if it's good it is truly wash-and-wear. The disadvantages are that knits snag badly, and they're quite warm, particularly if you keep your suit jacket on all day (as you should). They also always look like knits, and should be generally avoided for that reason. The measure of any business shirt is how well it imitates cotton, and the only men to whom I would recommend knits are those who must travel constantly and therefore must have the wash-and-wear advantage.

You can, if you are already very rich and very successful (in which case why are you reading this book?), or if you desire to have an affair with an Italian contessa, wear silk shirts. If you fit into neither of the above categories, then don't wear silk, I don't care how rich it makes you feel. A good silk shirt will cost you $50.00. Once you've paid for it, if the laundry doesn't ruin it on the first try, they will on the second. Silk very rarely has an acceptable look for business purposes; and when was the last time you heard of anyone asking for a raise wearing a $50.00 silk shirt?

Always avoid any shirt that has a shiny look to it, as well as all see-through weaves. No shiny shirt is acceptable for business wear anywhere, and while the see-through shirt is in excellent taste in parts of Europe, it is most certainly not so in the United States.

READY-MADES, SEMI-CUSTOMS AND FULL-CUSTOMS

There are three types of shirts you can buy, in terms of method of manufacture: mass-produced (or ready-made), semi-custom and full-custom. If you are easy to fit—if you can wear a standard collar size and common collar style, a standard sleeve length, and if you are neither too chunky nor too slim—then there is no compelling reason for you to buy anything other than ready-made shirts. These are certainly available in adequate variety and suitable quality at a number of price levels (generally, I would suggest that the average man pay no less than $10.00 and no more than $20.00 for a mass-produced shirt). You can buy a ready-made shirt one day and wear it the next. You don't have to buy any minimum quantity. And sometimes you can hit on a good sale.

Semi-custom shirts are exactly that, although almost never advertised as such. The stores that sell them would like you to believe you are getting a full-custom shirt, but you're not. At these stores, a number of measurements are taken and you are given a choice of materials and collar and cuff styles. Your shirts are then made up accordingly. Usually, the minimum order is four shirts, and delivery takes about six weeks.

The major advantage of the semi-custom is, obviously, fit. With ready-mades, you're limited to whole and half sizes for the collars and whole sizes for the sleeve lengths. And generally only God and the manufacturer know what the body size is. You also have to take whatever collar and cuff style you get. With semi-customs, the collars as well as the sleeves can be fitted as closely as quarter sizes; the shirt's body can be made to your individual requirements; and you have a wide choice of fabrics and styles.

The only problem is that they still aren't full-custom shirts. They are based on standard patterns (using the closest ones to what you need), cut on automatic cutters, and made in small factories. Don't get me wrong! I'm not knocking them, I only want you to know what you're getting. As a matter of fact, I wear them myself, and feel they offer the best shirt available for the money.

The prices start at about $16 and go up to about $30, depending on the fabrics you choose. And unless you have one shoulder much lower than the other, or some other physical abnormality that makes full-custom shirts a necessity, I would suggest semi-customs to anyone who can afford them, can buy four or more shirts at a time, and can wait six weeks or so for delivery.

The full-custom shirt, while it offers the ultimate luxury of absolutely individual tailoring and generally the finest fabrics available, is just not realistic for most men. Prices start at about $35.00; fittings are time-consuming; and since everything is done by hand specifically for you, delivery is rarely fast. In addition, given the realities of the typical laundry service, the luxury is just not worth the agony. Still, if you've got that kind of money to spend on clothes, there is no shirt to equal the full-custom.

HOW TO GET A GOOD FIT

No matter what type of shirt you wear, it should fit well. A surprising number of men really don't even know what size they need, and consequently there is always something just a little bit off with their shirts. You should have your shirt sizes taken at least once a year, by someone competent enough to do it right.

Obviously, in the less expensive stores, they probably won't even be able to find a tape measure, much less know how to use it. So find the most expensive store in your area and single out the most experienced-looking clerk. Have him take your measurements. If you can afford it, buy a shirt from him. If you can't afford it, and feel uncomfortable at having put him to the work without making a purchase, buy the shirt anyway. Then take it back the next day for a refund; say it didn't match your suit and you saw one down the street that goes perfectly.

The first area where a shirt should fit is around the waist. The shirt should be smooth all the way around, with no bagginess or bunching of material anywhere, but still loose enough to allow comfortable movement and to allow you to sit down without having the material pulling at the buttons.

The second area of fit is the length. A shirt should be long enough so that it does not pull up out of your pants during normal activity. When you buy a shirt, check the length; and when you find a comfortable one, stick with that brand and cut. Also important to the length, particularly if you are tall or chunky, is how many buttons a shirt has and where they are placed. The standard shirt has a six-button front, including the collar button. If you are tall or chunky and the bottom button hits you only an inch or so below the waist band of your pants, then after only the most minimum of activity, the button will slip out above the pants and the opening below it will spread apart, which looks awful.

If you have this problem, make sure the bottom button falls at least three inches below the waistband of your pants. If it doesn't, get an extra one sewn on. (Some moderately priced and almost all expensive ready-mades have a seven-button front, and you can always request it if you wear semi-customs.)

The third area of fit is the collar. This is the most crucial place, and also where most men are wearing the wrong size. They had the right size a year ago, but they've put on fifteen or so pounds, and now that size is too tight. The problem often is that it may not *feel* too tight, but it *looks* it—the collar wrinkles because of the tightness. This happens most frequently with soft collar shirts, such as Oxford cloths.

Usually middle-aged men wear their collars too tightly and men in their fifties, who are beginning to lose weight and get a few wrinkles in their necks, tend to wear them too loosely.

If you do wear semi-custom or full-custom shirts and have a wide choice of collar styles, you should also know that, ultimately, the height of the collar in the back should correspond to the length of your neck. A short collar on a man with a long neck emphasizes his problem, and a high collar on a man with a short neck makes him look like a turtle.

The height of the collar in the front depends almost entirely on age. If you're young, with no wrinkles, then the criterion should be how well a particular collar goes with your suit. If you're older and beginning to get wrinkles, get the collar up as high as looks decent to cover the wrinkles.

Collars should be spread in such a way as to be compatible with the lapels of your suit, and to hold the knot of your tie comfortably—with neither a lot of space showing (in which case the tie knot is too small for the collar spread) nor bulges (which means that the knot is too large for the spread).

While I'm on the subject of collars, I should also say that all dress shirts should have *removable* plastic collar stays. The only exception is for button-down-collar shirts, which should have a soft, natural look. Some cheap dress shirts and a lot of sport shirts are sold with sewn-in collar stays. The problem with them is that ironing the shirt with the stays in will leave ridges on the collar that outline the stays and often become shiny.

When you have removable stays, *always* take them out before sending your shirts to the laundry. If they're left in, the heat of commercial irons is so great that the stays can be fused to the collar and you can be left with a mess. Also, if you have a number of shirts with different length collars, make sure that you use the correct stays with each shirt. If the stays are too short for the collar, then they don't do what they were designed to do, and if the collar is not stiff enough, it will flop and curl. If the stays are too long and the back end is pressed tightly against the fold of the collar, they tend to create wrinkles or bulge against the material, showing their outline.

How to Maximize the Power of Shirts

The armholes of a properly fitting shirt should be open enough to allow comfortable movement, but if they're too open, so much material is required for the sleeves that the sleeves are baggy (this generally is not a problem with better shirts). The shoulder seams of shirts, those seams dividing the body of the shirt from the sleeves, should fall slightly over the edge of the shoulder bone, never more than one inch.

Shirt sleeves are measured from a point midway between the shoulders down to the wrists. Most men don't know this, and therefore don't understand why putting on a few pounds necessitates longer sleeves. When you are measured for a shirt, make sure that both arms are measured, not just one. If one arm is significantly longer than the other (and it is with a surprising percentage of men), you will have to wear semi-custom shirts to get the sleeves right.

The end of a shirt sleeve should come just a fraction below the wrist bone, and should extend about one-half inch below your suit jacket sleeve. (To get this right, always have the suit jacket adjusted to your shirt, not vice versa.)

Three inches is the standard length of the cuffs on business shirts. If you wear button cuffs, two buttons make for a smoother look than one, but this is a fairly insignificant point. If you wear French cuffs and cuff links (generally considered dressier than buttons), be prepared to get your shirts back from the laundry frequently with the cuffs folded and pressed wrong.

Button cuffs should fit as closely to the wrist as they can and still allow adequate movement. While we are discussing cuff buttons, there is one button that can be very important, and it is used to close the placket. This is the area above the cuff where the sleeve is split. This button, and its corresponding buttonhole, is normally found on better shirts and is always requested by those who know when buying a semi- or full-custom model. French cuffs should be slightly looser. Although a gentleman would never wear a bulky watch for business wear, this is sometimes a factor in how a cuff fits, so you should consider it.

When you are buying a shirt, every point mentioned above is important, because they all come together to give the correct total-fit you need. And although I won't tell you to measure every aspect of a shirt before buying it—mainly because I know you probably wouldn't take the trouble to do it—you should check those points that are most crucial to you.

PICKING PATTERNS AND COLORS

In any test, the most acceptable dress shirts—those that elicit the best responses for taste, class, credibility and effectiveness—are still, and will continue to be, white and solid colors. When properly color-coordinated or contrasted, solids go with every suit and every tie made. Of the solids, blue is the most popular, followed by the other pastels, the paler the better. A gaudy, loud yellow is not a good business shirt, but a pale, pastel yellow is.

If your principal business associates are over forty-five years old, if you must deal frequently with people from the lower-middle class (say you are a banker or a lawyer), never wear pink or pale lavender shirts, which have negative masculine associations. If you are black, avoid the same colors, as they have unfortunate but very real prejudicial associations. Never wear a solid red shirt, no matter who you are or what you do; it's just never acceptable.

If you have a sallow complexion, you should avoid any shade of gold, green or gray, colors which generally do not enhance anyone's facial coloration.

To avoid looking like a gangster, always make sure that your shirt is *lighter* than your suit, and your tie *darker* than your shirt (with some summer exceptions). In solid shirting, generally the paler, more subtle shade is the upper-middle-class one and the icy, shiny, darker, harsher color is the lower-middle-class symbol.

A very real practical historical basis exists for this. In earlier times, expensive shirts were made of superior quality materials, and the materials took dye very easily, which allowed for the lighter shades. Cheaper shirts were made of harder fabrics, more resistant to dye, and were mass-produced in far greater quantities. In order to dye them evenly at all, the dyes had to be dark and strong. Now, with improved dyeing techniques and fabrics, even cheaper shirts can approximate the pale colors of their more expensive counterparts, but the psychological class associations of color still remain.

When buying solid-color shirts, if you are on a budget and must buy as cheaply as possible, I suggest that you first go to the most expensive stores you can find. Look at the colors and textures of the best, most appropriate shirts, and then approximate them as closely as you can with shirts in your price range. With practice, you'll be able to do remarkably well, achieve the right look, and do it for what you can afford. As a matter of fact, you'll also be able to take some pride in bettering your more affluent counterparts: Any fool can get the proper look for twenty bucks a shirt, but it takes talent to do it for $8.50.

Several types of shirt are basically solid, but have a texture or pattern because the colored threads are interwoven with white threads. These are the end-on-end weave and the Oxford cloth, and both are not only highly acceptable shirts, they also add a richness, texture and variety to the solid look. (see drawing on page 60) In addition, end-on-ends and Oxford cloths, because of the white threading, are more acceptable in darker colors than is solid broadcloth.

Denim or chambray-look shirts also have the same type of weave and texture and are acceptable for some men in some professions. If you're not sure you should wear them, don't, and never wear them with very dressy suits.

A variation of the solid-color shirt is the pastel-colored shirt with white collar and/or cuffs. It is quite acceptable when worn with solid-color suits, provided you work in a high-fashion industry.

The second acceptable pattern in shirting is the simple stripe. (see drawing on page 61) The stripes may range from the very thin pinstripe to as wide as one-sixteenth of an inch. Some wider stripes might be acceptable, but unless you are sure, avoid

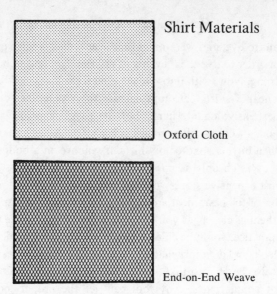

Shirt Materials

Oxford Cloth

End-on-End Weave

them. Generally, the closer the stripes are to each other, the more acceptable the shirt. As a general rule, if you are not dealing with the best material, avoid stripes if they are more than one-quarter inch apart.

The stripe can be of any color that coordinates or contrasts with the suit, as long as it is on a white background. As with solids, however, colors that are not flattering to the skin—gray, gold and green—should be avoided.

White stripes on a pastel background are acceptable for variety, but less so than the other way around. The darker the stripe, the more acceptable it is. For instance, my tests of a deep maroon show a higher acceptance than a bright red. The same is true of a dark blue versus a light blue.

Unless you really know what you are doing with striped shirts, the stripes should always be a single color, on a single color background. Some multicolored stripes are acceptable, but since there are so many variations of these, I cannot offer any hard rules. Basically, the multicolored stripe projects a lower-middle-class association in most people.

Shirt stripes should always be clearly defined and not have

Proper Business-Shirt Stripes

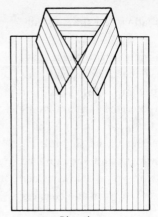

Pinstripe

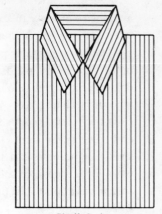

Chalk Stripe

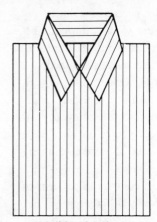

Traditional Stripe

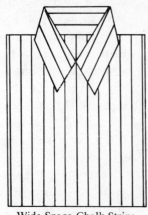

Wide-Space Chalk Stripe

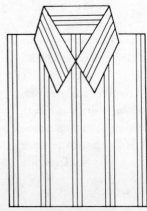

British Stripe

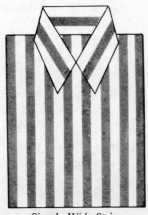

Simple Wide Stripe

a washed-out look. In striped patterns, all-cotton shirts usually offer a crisper effect than the blends.

The last acceptable pattern in a business shirt is the plaid—not a very heavy plaid, but a simple, delicate box plaid. (see drawing on page 63) When the plaid becomes a Glen plaid, or when it has a tartan or even a gingham look, the shirt automatically becomes a sport shirt. The rule for plaids, in both shirts and suits, is the same: Once it becomes even the slightest bit strong, it becomes strictly a sports garment and shouldn't be worn for business. In short, any plaid shirt you would consider wearing as a sport shirt probably shouldn't be worn as a business shirt.

For business wear, unacceptable shirt patterns far outnumber the acceptable ones. Unacceptable patterns include: any wavy stripe or ribbon weave; almost every satin pattern; almost every dot pattern; almost any highly woven or intricate pattern, particularly Jacquard including those described as the Jacquard stripe; and any pattern that tends to look washed out. As with stripes, multicolored shirts in any pattern are generally unacceptable, with the very nature of the colors tending toward lower-middle-class associations. Again, if you're not sure what you're doing, stay away from multicolored shirts (see drawing on page 64).

Everything I've said about materials, colors and patterns of shirts is based on years of testing in many different ways, but always with the same goals in mind: How successfully does this shirt project taste and class, and how effective is it in giving the wearer the look he should have for success in his particular undertaking? Since the successful dresser depends not only on specifics but also his combinations, we are generally talking about a total look (See Chapter 5), but here are several specific rules about shirts:

If you wish to create credibility with a man who is over fifty years old, you should wear a white shirt when dealing with him. If you wish to create credibility with a man in the upper echelons of industry, the most practical shirt is the pinstripe, dark blue being the preferable color, worn with a solid suit. These are

Two for Business, Four for Sport

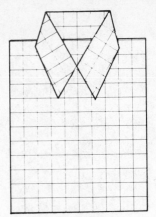

Business Box

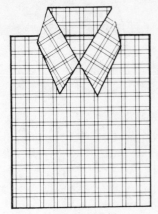

Business Plaid

Sport Box

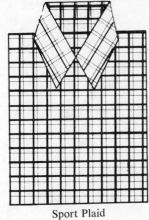

Sport Plaid

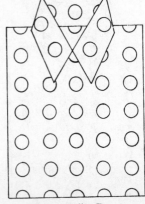

Sport Polka-Dot

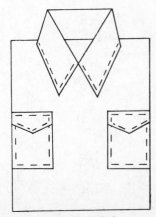

For Sport Only

Never for Business

Picture

Floral

Paisley

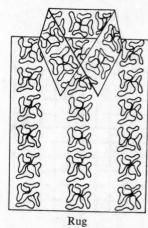

Rug

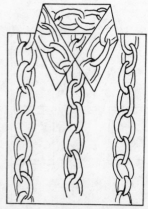

Chain

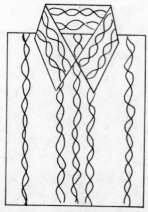

Ribbon

the shirts that my tests consistently prove to create the highest credibility and authority.

HOW ABOUT SHORT SLEEVES?

If you intend to take anything I've said in this book at all seriously, note well the following: You will never, ever, as long as you live, wear a short sleeve shirt for any business purpose, no matter whether you're the office boy or the president of the company.

In a study I conducted one summer several years ago, I used 200 executives, 100 who never wore short sleeve shirts, and 100 who frequently wore them. The study sought to determine whether long or short sleeves had any effect on the authority of the executive over his secretary's performance in terms of the amount of time she spent on the job. I set out to measure absenteeism, late arrivals to work and lunch hours that extended beyond the officially allotted time.

The differential for absenteeism was an insignificant one percent, but it was a bad time to test for this factor since most of the secretaries took their vacations in the summer and were less likely to stay home from work purposefully than they would have been in other periods when vacations provided no break. But the secretaries of those men who wore short sleeve shirts were late 12 percent more often than those who wore long sleeve shirts, and came back from lunch late *130 percent* more often.

Short sleeve shirts are symbols of the lower-middle class, and therefore pack no psychological authority or power. Upper-middle-class executives, who can afford good cotton long sleeve shirts and have air-conditioned offices, just do not wear short sleeve shirts, as well they shouldn't.

WHAT TO DO ABOUT MONOGRAMS

There's a funny story about monogrammed shirts. A young executive was having some custom shirts made and since monogramming was included in the price and he was something of a practical joker anyway, he had his monogrammed with the Chinese symbols for "No starch." In a word, he just liked the idea of a fancy extra, which is not unreasonable.

I personally find monograms somewhat ostentatious, but if you have reached the middle or upper levels of success, and like monograms, there's no reason not to have them. I suggest, however, that you use discreet, sophisticated lettering, no intricate scroll work, and that you have the monograms stitched on the left side about three inches above the belt line—in the European style—rather than way up on top of your nipple (see drawing below). Never have monograms put on your cuff.

Monograms

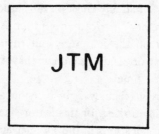

Simple,
Discreet Lettering
Works Best

Large,
Elaborate Lettering
Is in Poor Taste

WHAT ABOUT POCKETS?

One of the little ironies of our culture is that one of the marks of a very expensive dress shirt is that it usually has no pockets, because the man who can afford that shirt usually doesn't want or need the pocket. Obviously, if you must wear the less expensive ready-mades and the ones you can afford have pockets, you're stuck, although this should not be a matter of any great concern. But if you're buying expensive shirts, or semi- or full-customs, do get them without pockets, since they look much better. Under no circumstances should a dress shirt have two pockets. Shirt pockets should be of the simple patch type, with no flap or button.

NO-NO DETAILS

No dress shirt should have epaulets or decorative pleats or cowboy yokes or be sewn with thread that is different in color from that of the shirt fabric. Buttons should be plain and simple and usually white.

HERE'S A BASIC SHIRT WARDROBE

One certain way to buy shirts will insure that you always have what you need: Every time you buy a suit, immediately buy shirts (and ties) to wear with that suit. Too many men say to themselves, "Well, I'll get this suit, but I have shirts and ties already." When the suit comes, the existing shirts and ties usually don't go well together but are worn anyway.

The result is that the total look is inappropriate, and no matter how careful a man has been in selecting the suit, if everything doesn't blend, the effort is wasted. Other men buy shirts on impulse, frequently guessing that they will match some suit at home, which they generally don't. The result is a bad combination and an unsuccessful look.

The number of shirts you should have for each suit depends almost entirely on how frequently you must wear the suit and how fast your laundry is. I would suggest three shirts (and two ties) as the absolute minimum for each suit. The more suits you have, the fewer shirts you will need for each one, and the more shirts you will have that will go well with several different suits, but that in no way eliminates the need always to buy shirts for specific suits rather than trying to buy one shirt to go with more than one suit.

Assuming that your basic suit wardrobe is the usual mix of

grays, blues and browns, I suggest the following as a basic shirt wardrobe, given that the appropriate shades of color are chosen for each suit:

1 dressy, solid-white broadcloth, to be worn regularly.

1 dressy, solid-white broadcloth, to be kept in a plastic bag, clean, ironed and always ready for emergencies. After a year, or as needed, buy a new emergency shirt and make the old one your everyday white shirt.

1 solid-white Oxford cloth with button-down collar.

3 solid-blue broadcloth shirts.

2 blue end-on-end weaves.

2 blue Oxford cloths with button-down collars.

2 dark blue pinstripes on white background.

1 maroon pinstripe on white background.

1 brown pinstripe on white background.

2 solid-beige broadcloths.

1 solid-pale-yellow broadcloth.

1 pale yellow Oxford cloth with button-down collar.

6 other shirts in any colors or patterns (other than the forbidden ones) according to your taste and needs.

4.

HOW TO PICK YOUR
MOST IMPORTANT STATUS
SYMBOLS: YOUR TIES

Several years ago, as an adjunct to my consulting work, I operated a small shirt and tie store for the benefit of my clients. Since suitable shirts and ties seemed to be the most difficult items of apparel for them to find and match correctly on their own, it was much simpler for me to provide them rather than to waste hours shopping with my clients in other stores.

One day, while in the store alone, two stick-up men robbed me. In addition to the small amount of cash I had on hand, they took a quantity of ties. I have no idea what they *thought* they'd get from me, but a handful of ties, no matter how elegant and expensive, just didn't seem worth the risk they were taking.

Following the robbery, I went to the police precinct to look at mug shots of known stick-up men operating in the area. Although I could not identify the ones who hit me, after going through about one thousand pictures, one fact stuck in my mind. None of the stick-up men was wearing a tie—in a precinct of midtown Manhattan which contains, among other features, probably the greatest number of suit-and-tie businessmen per square block than anywhere else in the world. Didn't the stick-up men know that their chances of success and escape would be immensely improved if they could blend in with their surroundings? Intrigued, I asked the desk sergeant if the cops ever arrested anyone wearing a tie. "Hardly ever," was his reply.

On the other hand, as I looked around the station house, every detective I saw was wearing a tie—not the immaculately-knotted, perfectly-coordinated, upper-middle-class symbols worn by the dashing detectives on "Kojak," but ties nonetheless. One officer, who was obviously some kind of undercover man dressed to look like a bum on the street, put his tie on when he came into the station house.

That anecdote illustrates the point I want to make: The tie is probably the single most important denominator of social status for a man in the United States today. Show me a man's ties and I will tell you who he is, or who he is trying to be.

Still, if you are like most men, you actually pay very little *conscious* attention to your ties. And some of you will say, "It isn't my tie that's significant, but my car, my home, the size of my bank account, the quality of my art collection, the contents of my liquor closet, the amount of jewelry my wife has, etc., etc."

Don't you believe it—not during your working hours anyway. Those things are all fine; they'll make you very comfortable in life. But if I'm in a business meeting with you; if you're trying to sell me something; if I'm a juror listening to your defense of a client, I'm not going to see the extraneous things. I'm going to see *you;* I'm going to see how you are dressed. And whether you like it or not, or believe it or not, your tie, more than any other aspect of your appearance, will determine how I and other people view your status, credibility, personality and ability.

Because I learned very early in my research that ties are so important, I have probably conducted more experiments with them and more testing of them than I have with any other articles of clothing. Running through this entire litany of experiments would be boring and out of place in this book, but a small sample is in order.

Your Most Important Status Symbols: Your Ties

In one set of experiments, I asked a group of men to apply for jobs that were available and for which they were reasonably qualified. For some interviews, they would go properly dressed, in suit and tie. For others, I instructed them not to wear ties, but to say that they had their tie in their hand, stopped for a cup of coffee, left the tie on the counter, and did not go back to get it since they didn't want to be late for the interview.

Invariably, those men who wore their ties to interviews were offered jobs; those without them were turned down. And in one almost incredible situation, the interviewer (the president of a small corporation) was made so uncomfortable by the applicant's lack of a tie that he gave the man $6.50, told him to go out and buy a tie, put it on, and then come back to complete the interview. He still didn't get the job.

In another set of experiments, six men were asked to have dinners in various upper-middle-class restaurants with their wives. On some occasions, they wore suits but no ties; on others, they were properly attired. On each occasion, whenever the check was presented, they said to the restaurant manager that they had left their wallet with cash and credit cards at home, and asked to pay by personal check. When they were wearing ties, their checks were graciously accepted; without ties, they were in many instances refused, and the wife was forced to use the pre-planned emergency solution: "Oh, wait a minute, I think I may have enough cash to cover this."

In twenty-seven restaurants in New York where ties are not mandatory attire, I asked the headwaiter or *maître d'* to divide the room into two simple sections—more preferable seating areas and less preferable seating areas. Inevitably, those areas near the street door and kitchen door were considered to be the less preferable. I then spent a number of evenings observing the seating procedures at peak dinner hours of those restaurants. Invariably, there was a disproportionate number of men without ties in the less preferable areas, and almost no men without ties in the more preferable areas.

To determine how people feel about tie-wearers in strictly

economic terms, I took twin pictures of the same man. In one, he was wearing a nondescript gray suit and tie; in the other he wore a similar suit, but with no tie and an open-collar shirt. Over one hundred people picked at random were asked to estimate the yearly income of each of the two "twins." Although there are obviously numerous variations in such surveys, the "twin" wearing the tie was generally awarded $3000 to $4000 more per year than his "brother."

Using the same set of photos, but questioning only women, I asked which of the men the women would trust enough to let into their homes, provided they didn't know him. Sixty percent of the women trusted neither, but of the forty percent who trusted one of them, they chose the man with the tie almost without exception.

In an experiment that I enjoyed more than any other, I panhandled money around the Port Authority Bus Terminal and Grand Central Station in New York. My approach was to stop people, say I was terribly embarrassed, but had left my wallet home, and needed 75 cents to get home. I did this for two hours at rush hour. During the first hour, I wore a suit, but no tie; for the second hour, I added my tie. In the first hour, I made $7.23, but in the second, with my tie on, I made $26.00, and one man even gave me extra money for a newspaper.

No question, then: The tie is a symbol of respectability and responsibility; it communicates to other people who you are, or reinforces or detracts from their conception of who you should be. While the most appropriate tie, worn correctly, naturally cannot insure your success in business or in life, it certainly can —and should—give off the right signals to keep you from being regarded as a no-class boob.

HOW TO BUY TIES

Buying ties is relatively simple, once you know the rules and adhere to them. But it isn't as simple as telling your wife, girlfriend or secretary to pick you up a few at lunch. That's the worst thing you could do. Unless the lady in question is exceptional, she's going to see you in a different light from that of your business associates; she's probably going to brighten you up to fulfill *her* image of how you should dress and look. And that will, a lot more times than not, spell disaster at the office. Unless you'd ask your wife, girlfriend or secretary to write your next report to the boss, don't ask her to buy your ties.

Accept the fact that buying and wearing ties correctly is a very serious matter, one that requires time, effort and thought. And do it yourself; I guarantee that it will pay off.

The first thing you should do before buying ties is to determine what length they should be. There is little that looks worse on a man than a tie that is either too long or too short. When tied properly, the tip of the tie should come just to your belt buckle, no more, no less (see drawing on page 74). What length you will need will therefore depend on how tall you are and how you knot your tie (see drawings on pages 75–78 for the most common knotting methods).

There is, strangely, a tremendous variation in the length of ties, with better ties tending to be longer. The standard lengths are fifty-five or fifty-six inches. Take a tie that fits you properly, measure it, and when you buy a new one, make sure that it's of a comparable length.

The width of a tie is also important, and although there is no firm and fast math that can be used to determine the proper width with a given suit, basically the width of the tie should be harmonious with the width of the suit lapels. At the present, standard tie widths are from four to four and one-half inches at the widest end.

Next, it is important that the tie make a good knot. To do so, it must have substance, which is provided by a lining of coarse material sewn into the tie, as well as the material from which the tie itself is made. Cheap polyesters and shiny silks slip quite badly, and light, thin silks do not offer enough substance, unless they are heavily lined. In addition to the coarse inner

Proper Tie Length and Proper Fitting Belt

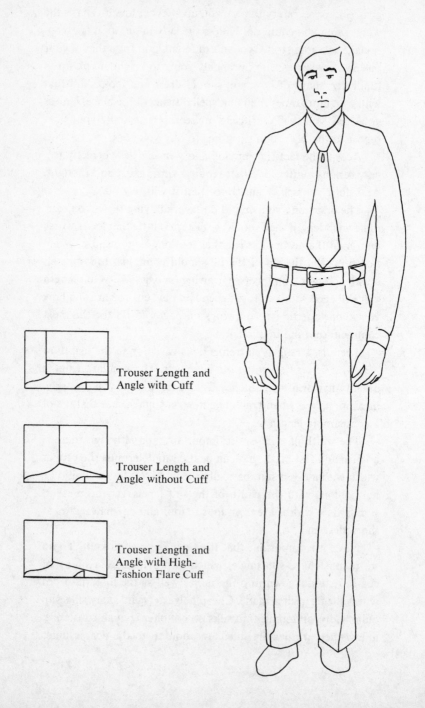

Trouser Length and Angle with Cuff

Trouser Length and Angle without Cuff

Trouser Length and Angle with High-Fashion Flare Cuff

HOW TO TIE A TIE

The Windsor Knot
Wide and triangular—for wide-spread shirt collars.

Your Left
in Mirror

Your Right
in Mirror

1
Start with wide end of tie on your right and extending a foot below narrow end.

2
Cross wide end over narrow and bring up through loop.

3
Bring wide end down, around behind narrow, and up on your right.

4
Then put down through loop and around across narrow as shown.

5
Turn and pass up through loop and . . .

6
Complete by slipping down through the knot in front. Tighten and draw up snug to collar.

The Half-Windsor Knot
Medium symmetrical triangle—for standard shirt collars.

1
Start with wide end of tie on your right and extending a foot below narrow end.

2
Cross wide end over narrow and turn back underneath.

3
Bring up and turn down through loop.

4
Pass wide end around front from left to right.

5
Then, up through loop . . .

6
And down through knot in front. Tighten carefully and draw up to collar.

The Four-in-Hand Knot
Long and straight—to complement a standard shirt collar.

1
Start with wide end of tie on your right and extending a foot below narrow end.

2
Cross wide end over narrow, and back underneath.

3
Continue around, passing wide end across front of narrow once more.

4
Pass wide end up through loop.

5
Holding front of knot loose with index finger, pass wide end down through loop in front.

6
Remove finger and tighten knot carefully. Draw up tight to collar by holding narrow end and sliding knot up sung.

The Bow Tie

1
Start with end
in left hand
extending
1½″ below
that in right
hand.

2
Cross longer
end over
shorter and
pass up
through loop.

3
Form front
loop of bow
by doubling up
shorter end
(hanging) and
placing across
collar points.

4
Hold this front
loop with
thumb and
forefinger of
left hand. Drop
long end down
over front.

5
Place right
forefinger,
pointing up,
on bottom half
of hanging
part. Pass up
behind front
loop and . . .

6
Poke resulting
loop through
knot behind
front loop (see
illustration).
Even ends and
tighten.

lining, the tie should also be fully lined or backed with a light, but good quality material.

Since all types of tie pins or tie clasps are not now considered in good taste, a tie should have a tab on the back of the large end, into which the smaller end may be slipped so that it doesn't stick out from the back of the tie.

HOW TO PICK TIE MATERIALS

The best material for ties is silk; the next best is polyester that looks like silk, or polyester and silk combinations, which are excellent. Then comes wool and, finally, cotton.

There are three main types of silk tie, the lightest being the foulard silk. The foulard is a fine, elegant tie, and the only problem with it, already mentioned, is that it must be substantially lined if it's going to make a good knot and keep it.

Next there is the regular, or normal weave, silk tie. There are a lot of names for this one; I call it the solid silk. It really doesn't matter what you call it if you understand that it's the tie everyone immediately thinks of when you mention silk ties. It's usually a solid color; it's shiny, but doesn't glisten; and it can be worn with almost anything, anywhere.

Last is the woven silk tie, and this one is very tricky. Sometimes men go out to treat themselves and spend $25.00 for a tie, getting the very best woven silk and the very best heavy lining. The problem is that it's very difficult to get a good knot with it because it's so heavy. So, while you must be sure that the lining inside a foulard is heavy enough, conversely, you must be sure that the lining inside a woven silk is light enough to insure a proper knot.

When buying a silk tie, you should pay at least $6.50 for it, usually more (unless you're buying in a sale). Anything cheaper will look terrible after several wearings, even if it looks okay when you buy it. There is really no top limit to what silk ties can cost, but the very best ties in the best stores run well under $25.00. If a tie costs more, then you're paying for something other than quality.

There is only one rule about an all-polyester tie; if it looks like a good silk, buy it. If not, don't. The only characteristic of polyester in ties is how well it imitates silk. The average price range for a good polyester tie is between $5 and $8. Good polyester ties tend to stand up to wear better than silks in the same price range, and can even look better after dry cleaning than expensive silk. Blends of polyester and silk are generally the best buy if you are budget conscious because they offer the rich look of silk and the durability of polyester. These are less expensive than silk, and hold up quite well.

There are three primary types of wool tie. First is the knitted tie, which is usually a fairly sporty tie, and should be worn accordingly. All knitted ties should be wool; if they are made from an artificial fiber, they should look and feel like wool.

The woven wool tie has a very bushy look to it and is made from the same types of material one would associate with the heaviest winter sport jackets.

Knitted and woven wool ties must be very carefully measured so that they will not be too short when tied; will make a neat knot; and will not be so thick that they cause the shirt collar to bulge. Usually, a simple overhand knot is the only one that will work successfully.

Because they are at best more bulky than other ties, knitted and woven wool ties should be generally avoided by heavy men with large necks and oval faces since the ties will only emphasize the very physical characteristics that they would be wise to deemphasize. However, these are probably the most durable of ties, and will last for years, even after many dry cleanings. Some of them can even be washed in Woolite, although there is a danger that the lining (if the tie has one) might shrink in disproportion to the tie material.

The last major category of wool tie is the wool challis. It is a finer, smoother weave, and is backed and lined exactly like silk. In fact, the challis very often has almost the same look and design of silk, with the exception that it is not at all shiny, which makes it less formal. It is useful because it tends to wear, dry-clean and travel better than silk.

Cotton ties are worn year-round in the South and elsewhere in the summer. The best way to determine whether a cotton tie is good is how much you pay for it. It should be no less than $5.00 or more than $10.00. If you pay less than $5.00, you're getting a cheap cotton that won't hold up, and if you pay more than $10.00 you're being cheated, because no cotton tie is worth more.

Although cotton is such a versatile fabric that it can be woven to look like almost any other material, the predominant look in cotton ties is light in both weight and color. Because of the light colors, it is advisable to Scotchguard cotton ties simply by spraying them.

Linen ties are beautiful, but stay away from them unless you can afford to buy them to wear only a few times. Linen wrinkles incredibly, and the wrinkles are virtually impossible to remove.

There are some materials from which ties should never be made. The main one is acetate. Never buy an acetate tie; it's a piece of junk. Likewise, don't buy rayon, which will not hold its shape longer than several wearings, and even when it's new it does not yield the rich look that an acceptable tie must have.

HOW TO SELECT PATTERNS OF TIES

There are almost as many patterns of ties as there are crystal formations in snowflakes, but only a few are suitable for the businessman who has reached the top or is trying to. This statement is not as restrictive as it sounds; there is still a tremendous variety to be found in color combinations, material and textures.

The most obvious pattern for a tie, the one that is the most useful generally, is no pattern at all. In other words, a solid. The reason is simple: A solid tie will go with any patterns in any suits or shirts. It is the perfect—and sometimes the only—sensible complement to the very loud shirt, say a broad plaid or heavy stripe, and to any suit.

A lot of men believe they shouldn't wear a solid tie with a solid suit and solid shirt, but that is nonsense. A combination of solids is perfectly acceptable if the colors and textures are properly coordinated—say a gray suit, a light blue shirt and a wine tie. If you wear very expensive clothes, then combinations of solids tend to emphasize the qualities of the materials and tailoring, by not giving the eye extraneous details to focus on. Of course, you probably would not wish to wear all solids every day.

For a basic tie wardrobe, I suggest that every man have at least a solid blue tie, and one other solid from the following: brown, beige or maroon, depending on his wardrobe, possibly all of them if affordable. The man with an extensive wardrobe should also have several light, summer, pastel solids, a gray solid, and maybe even a white. I don't like white solids myself —there is always the problem of keeping them clean—but it is an acceptable tie in certain situations.

There are solid-color ties that have a raised pattern on them. Usually these are made from polyester but can be made from silk. The worst of these, generally the cheaper polyesters, are hideously garish even if the colors are the most conservative. If you like this type of tie, my only suggestions are to make sure the raised patterns are subtle, and I suggest that you go for the most expensive you can afford, preferably silk.

The next pattern we find in ties is the evenly spaced, repeating pattern. The best known of these is, of course, the polka-dot, a small round dot repeated in regular intervals against a solid background. The polka-dot tie is almost as versatile as the solid and there is, in my experience, no tie more elegant. The background color of a polka-dot tie is dominant, and should either match or contrast with the suit color. The dot should pick up the color of the shirt.

The most common polka-dot tie is dark blue with a white dot, and the reason is traditional. Years ago the *de rigueur* "uniform" for the upper-middle-class executive was a dark blue suit and white shirt. The tie picked up both colors perfectly, and presented a stunning, crisp, dignified look, as it still does.

You can buy polka-dot ties with dots as big as marbles, but

generally speaking, the smaller the dots, the more sophisticated and dressy the tie (see drawing below).

Also in the category of the evenly spaced, repeating pattern tie is the classic club tie with its small heraldic shields against a solid background—and its derivation, which I call the itty bitty fishy tie. It features, against its mandatory solid background, some emblem of traditionally upper-class sports: a little fish with a fly in its mouth, a tennis racquet, a sailboat, a golf

Proper Business Ties

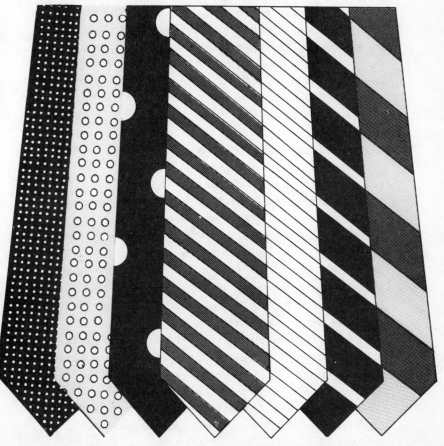

Polka-Dot   Rep

ball or club, a horse or polo bat, etc. You will find these ties in all the best stores, and they sell with great consistency.

They go with almost any conservatively patterned shirt and certainly with every solid. Generally, it would not be advisable to wear the club tie or its derivations with any strongly patterned shirt, since the emblem on the tie will clash with the strong pattern more times than not. And even if it doesn't, it is very often inappropriate to wear a conservative tie against a wild shirt.

The next acceptable tie pattern is the rep, or regimental rep, which is the traditional tie of the American businessman. Technically, "rep" means a ribbed or corded fabric, but a rep tie is, quite simply, a diagonally striped tie. Originally, the regimental rep was designed to represent whatever British regiment a gentleman served in, and each had its own distinctive stripe and coloration. There are only about 40 true regimental ties, but about 400 imitations, all of which are acceptable in this category.

The only rules for the rep tie are that the stripes must be neat, clean and generally of dark colors. For summer, the stripes are pastel against a white background, and this is the accepted summer rep of the upper-middle class.

The next category of acceptable tie pattern is what I call the foulard, because that is the type of silk it is usually found in. Many people refer to this as the Ivy League tie, since the pattern says Daddy went to Yale, Grandad went to Yale, and we hope little Junior will go to Yale also. It's a tie that traditionally indicated that the wearer was not only of a certain class, but that he also belonged to an elite social group. It represented Boston and Palm Beach society, Harvard, Yale, and Princeton.

There are several variations of the Ivy League tie, but generally it features a small rounded triangle or irregular circle with variations inside. Whatever the designs (see drawing on page 85), they are always crisp, neat, and repeated on fine silk.

An offshoot of the foulard is the repeating diamond pattern (see drawing on page 85). As with the polka-dot, the smaller the

| Club | Club | Ivy League | Ivy League | Repeating Diamond | Paisley | Basic Plaid |

diamonds are, the more sophisticated is the tie. This is probably the best tie for a man in an authority position, since it says he is conservative and upper class to the members of the upper class without turning off the lower-middle class with which the man might come in contact (if he is a banker or lawyer, for example). The traditional Ivy League tie, because of its prior associations, does tend to turn off the lower-middle class.

The paisley tie is the sporty tie of the upper-middle class. I call it the upper-middle-class amoeba run wild, since if you took an amoeba, painted it in multiple colors, expanded its size and threw sixty together, you would have a paisley pattern (see drawing on page 85).

Being basically a sporty tie, the paisley has certain limitations. It is not considered a serious tie, and unlike the patterns previously discussed, should not be worn to the most serious business meetings. But it is an excellent tie to wear with a dull suit. Picking up the color of a dull suit with a bright paisley tie presents a stunning effect; in fact, the basic use of the paisley tie is to blend a total look—suit, shirt and tie—together.

The paisley is one of the cleverest ties you can take with you when traveling, and is also quite good for men on strict budgets, since it contains so many colors that one tie can match several suits.

The paisley pattern is one that you will find mixed with almost every other acceptable tie pattern. It moves over into club tie derivations, with small colorful amoebas repeated in evenly spaced patterns against a solid background. When the amoebas are even smaller, it becomes a derivation of the Ivy League tie, and when the amoebas alternate with stripes, it becomes a hybrid of the rep tie. The hybrids, particularly the club and Ivy League variations, may be worn as you would wear their slightly more conservative counterparts.

Acceptable plaid ties fall into two categories. They are either heavy woolen plaids that go extremely well with the bushy, soft flannel suit, or they are the linen or cotton plaids, usually of light pastel colors, for summer wear.

TIES THAT SHOULD NEVER BE WORN

The best rule for avoiding ties that may convey the wrong look and the wrong associations is: Unless you are sure of what you are doing, wear nothing other than those I have recommended on the preceding pages. But I can also give you some specifics. Never wear anything gaudy except a paisley. Never wear ties with large symbols. Never wear "storybook" or "big picture" ties, I don't care what the prevailing fashion is. Avoid any material that shows signs of poor dyeing, which is usually evidenced by harsh lower-middle-class colors, washed out patterns or colors or patterns that run into each other. Avoid anything that is unusual in color, pattern, shape or size. I once saw a tie that consisted of a loose red knit enclosing a black lace background. You wouldn't wear that one. Avoid any tie that is too short. Avoid black ties unless you are going to a funeral. Avoid purple under all circumstances. And avoid any pattern that is just hard to look at.

WHAT TO DO ABOUT BOW TIES

For business wear bow ties give off several negative effects. You will not be taken seriously when wearing one. The only positive use comes if you are too powerful a personality, in which case they can soften your image. But otherwise you will not be thought responsible if you wear a bow tie. Most people will not trust you with anything important. It is a death knell for anyone selling his services as a consultant or lawyer, etc. The number of people who will trust you at all, with anything, will be cut in half.

In general, I have found that people believe that a man in a bow tie will steal. It creates the impression of being unpredictable, thus some experienced trial lawyers who believe they have a good case will try to keep a man wearing a bow tie off a jury.

Bow ties are acceptable as sports attire, and if you do wear them for such occasions, stick to the same patterns recommended for all other ties.

5.

PUTTING YOUR OWN LOOK
ALL TOGETHER

A few years ago, I received a call from the owner of one of Connecticut's most successful and most prestigious men's clothing stores. He said he had a problem and he came right out with it: he had no taste. He had buyers who chose the clothing for the store, and even though he never attempted to wait on customers, he was seen around the premises and known as the owner and felt he needed to dress well. He had been hiring a "fashion consultant" to put his clothing together, but recently he had received some negative comments on how he looked.

When I met him at his home, I found a selection of clothing only slightly smaller than that in his store. But when I looked at the combinations his "fashion consultant" had recommended, I realized that the consultant had been dressing him directly from the pages of *Gentlemen's Quarterly*. The problem was that this man was six feet, four inches tall and weighed 240 pounds, hardly a size compatible with the tricky combinations and style of high-fashion clothing. Not to mention that the clothing seen in such magazines is rather atypical of the clothes worn in a suburban Connecticut town.

I suggested that the man change his wardrobe, and because he could do so from his store, he immediately began wearing the combinations I had suggested. Several weeks later, when I went back to see how he was doing, the man said he felt much more comfortable and had received a number of compliments on his new look.

A year later, however, he was back to wearing high-fashion horse blankets. When I asked him why, he said I was a nice fellow and all that, but had charged him only $150 for my advice. His "fashion consultant" always charged him $500, and everyone knows that a $500 consultant is better than a $150 consultant. Not wishing to argue with such logic, I told the man he was absolutely correct and immediately raised my prices.

The clothing combinations I recommend for business wear do not come from the pages of men's fashion magazines. Neither are they determined by my own personal opinions. They are the result of research and testing, and they reflect the conscious and unconscious reactions of a valid cross section of the American public. They work because the American public says that these clothes, in these combinations, project a look of good taste, of credibility, and of upper-middle class success.

The fact that the colors, patterns and combinations of clothing that score the highest positive results among the largest majority of the population are all traditional and conservative should come as no great surprise. Familiarity, at least in the senses, does not breed contempt; it breeds acceptance. The most successful businessmen have for years worn conservative clothing, and will for many more years.

When I first began testing, my method was to photograph a dozen men in conservative, well-matched colors and patterns. Another dozen men were photographed in well-matched, but more modern clothing—the type generally seen in fashion magazines. When the two dozen photos were jumbled together and shown in no particular order, 70 to 80 percent of my population sample chose the men in conservative dress as more tasteful than the men in more modern garb. This figure held true even though 40 to 50 percent of the men being questioned did not dress conservatively themselves. Even when 70 to 80 percent of the men being questioned personally dressed in more modern colors and patterns and styles, their answers never substantially changed the statistical breakdown of the study.

When I discovered this familiarity effect, I tested it further, using shirts and ties. I made one grouping of ten shirts and ties that were strictly traditional; and another grouping of ten shirts and ties that were nontraditional, but not gaudy. Within the two separate groups, ties were indiscriminately placed on shirts. I then asked 300 people to judge whether each combination was in good taste, poor taste or neutral. Those were the only choices.

After every ten people had answered, I again indiscriminately combined the shirts and ties within their separate groups. Eighty-seven percent of the people chose the largest majority of the traditional combinations as in good taste. Seventy percent of the same people chose the more modern combinations as being in poor taste.

Then, arming myself with a large number of photographs of suit, shirt and tie combinations that I believed should be acceptable to most people, I first showed these photographs to large numbers of people who were identifiably upper-middle class. These people were asked to identify the combination as tasteful or average. Any combination that was chosen by over half of the people questioned as being average was considered unacceptable.

With the most important business combinations, my testing was far more complex. With photographs of men wearing various combinations, I asked a cross section of the population to identify the efficient man, the hard worker, the good family man, the banker, the plumber, etc. Whenever any combination turned up in a negative category with a consistency of better than one-third, it was discarded, and I do not recommend it.

Putting Your Own Look All Together

HOW TO TAKE THE HEADACHE OUT OF COORDINATING CLOTHES

When you coordinate clothing, there are only four serious elements of concern: the colors, the lines, the textures and the styles.

In choosing color, men make two basic mistakes. They either wear colors that clash or colors that are so monochromatic that they fade into each other. A light gray suit with a pale blue shirt and a pale blue tie is an example of colors that fade, while an orange tie and a green shirt with a blue suit is an obvious and absurd clash of colors, but is, in effect, not a lot worse than some combinations I have seen otherwise astute businessmen wear.

The lines of any garment are the directions in which the pattern runs. A pinstripe suit has a vertical pattern. A plaid suit has both a vertical and a horizontal pattern. A paisley tie has a nondirectional pattern. Some club ties have diagonal patterns; rep ties have diagonal patterns. When putting clothing together, it is very important that a pattern that travels in one direction is not put next to a pattern that travels in another direction; the lines will clash.

Texture is a concern that is generally overlooked, but it can be used to match materials with very pleasing effect. A nice, heavy wool tie with a heavy flannel suit or a linen tie with a linen suit are good textural combinations. Very seldom is there a serious clash of textures, but it can happen occasionally, such as if a silk shantung tie is worn with a heavy flannel suit.

All items of clothing have a definite, identifiable style. Pinstripe suits, for example, have a conservative, businesslike style, and it would be a severe clash of styles to wear a sporty shirt with a pinstripe suit. Similarly, a narrow, traditionally patterned tie would look silly if worn with a wide-lapeled, high-fashion suit. The combination of styles must be appropriate.

The simplest, effective and always acceptable combination of clothing is solids. The classic mistake most men make about solids is that they think they are dull, or that solids should not be combined. Both thoughts are ludicrous. If, in the combination of three solids—suit, shirt and tie—any one of the three is very lively, your outfit will not be dull. If you use contrast in addition—for instance, combining a dark blue suit, a white shirt and a maroon tie—you will project a sharp, fashionable look. If you see a man with three solids well put together, you can almost be sure that he is an excellent dresser, and that he accomplishes his look with the least effort. Poor dressers struggle to put patterns together and rarely succeed.

Because of its great flexibility, with patterns as well as with other solids, the solid suit should be the staple of every man's wardrobe. The most acceptable colors for solid suits are blue, gray and beige. All of these test well in almost any combinations, and they are the three solids I recommend to every client.

A solid suit may be worn with a shirt of almost any pattern, and if this is followed up with a solid tie, as I have shown in Pictures 1 and 2, it always yields a workable combination. This combination—solid, pattern, solid—follows one of the first rules I offer any client who has trouble matching clothes: Never put two patterns together. If you are not sure of what you are doing, always separate patterns by a solid.

Pictures 1 and 2 also demonstrate another aspect of matching the solid suit with the patterned shirt. In Picture 1, we have a solid gray suit, a maroon striped shirt, and a solid gray tie which picks up the color of the suit. In Picture 2, we have a solid gray suit, a maroon plaid shirt, and a maroon tie, which picks up the color of the shirt. In both cases, I have used the tie to pick up one of the color elements in the already existing combination of suit and shirt because those combinations have enough life in them.

If the suit and shirt combinations were dull, I would choose a contrasting tie to liven the look. For example, if the second gray suit, which has a tinge of blue in it, were worn with a pale blue shirt, it would be a bit dull. I would therefore give life to the combination with a maroon tie.

With solid suits, we may also wear solid shirts and patterned ties, because patterns as well as colors liven the look. In Pictures 3 and 4, we have two solid-blue suits worn with white shirts for contrast. Silk foulard ties pick up the white shirt alone in Picture 4 and, in Picture 3, both the white shirt and the blue suit.

So with the solid suit, there are three basic acceptable combinations: solid suit with solid shirt and solid tie; solid suit with patterned shirt and solid tie; and solid suit with solid shirt and patterned tie.

Although I don't recommend it to anyone until he has acquired a real feel for matching clothes, it is also possible to wear a solid suit with a patterned shirt and a patterned tie, particularly if the two patterns are traditional, and one of them is nondirectional or very soft and quiet. For example, if we take a solid suit and put a pinstripe shirt with it, we can use almost any tie on that shirt, since the pinstripe is usually not strong enough to create contrast, even with a rep tie.

For an entirely different reason, we may sometimes wear a rep tie with a chalk-stripe shirt and a solid suit. Although there is a strong contrast of line, it does not strike us as being negative since we have been conditioned by seeing this combination on successful businessmen so often that we accept it as a common upper-middle-class combination.

Just as there is little problem in matching the solid suit, the problems with matching the pinstripe suit are also almost nonexistent. The only element that goes with the solid suit but not the pinstripe is the plaid shirt. The plaid clashes with the vertical line of the stripe, and it also clashes in effect because the plaid shirt tends to be a bit sporty while the pinstripe suit tends to be very serious and businesslike.

The pinstripe suit will always be appropriate with a solid shirt, although the only two shirt colors I recommend are pale blue and white. Some other colors may sometimes work, but white and blue are best. They are compatible with the serious, businesslike style, and since acceptable pinstripe suits normally have either a white or blue stripe, the use of a same-color shirt tends to bring out the stripe and give the suit more life. Picture 6 is an excellent example of this. The white shirt picks up the white stripe in the suit and gives it a very crisp, clean look.

It is also possible to combine a pinstripe suit with a pinstripe shirt, mainly because both stripes are usually so weak that they do not conflict with each other, or even affect one another. It is even possible, as I show in Picture 3, to use the pinstripe suit in three-pattern combinations, here a pinstripe suit, a pinstripe shirt and a nondirectional tie. Again, unless you are absolutely sure of what you are doing, I don't suggest you attempt such combinations; keep to only two patterns whenever possible.

The strength of the pinstripe in a suit effects the shirts and ties that can be worn with it. An example of this is Picture 7, in which we have a rep tie with the diagonal lines obviously clashing with the pinstripes. Yet the pinstripes are so weak that the clash is not noticeable, and here the rep tie works well with a pinstripe suit. When tested with stronger pinstripes, the rep tie does not work well at all, and is looked upon by a sizeable percentage of the population as being in poor taste.

With the pinstripe suit and solid shirt, the preferable tie patterns are nondirectional, such as the Ivy League (see Pictures 3 and 4), the club (see Picture 15) or the polka-dot (see Picture 6).

The most difficult acceptable suit pattern to match is, as you might expect, the plaid, because of its multidirectional lines. The only acceptable shirts that can be worn with plaid suits are solids, with no exceptions. The only ties that can be worn with the plaid suit are nondirectional—paisley, polka-dot, solid, club or Ivy League—or, in some cases, other plaids.

Shirts and ties perform several secondary functions with plaid suits. The first is to liven up a dull plaid. Picture 9 shows a rather dull blue suit to which I have added a light blue shirt which picks up the light blue lines in the suit. The gray and light blue tie again picks up the light blue lines in the suit. This causes the shirt and tie to interact with the suit, to give it more life and make an acceptable combination.

The plaid suit in Picture 10 is an average business plaid. It does display one definite upper-middle-class characteristic that I wish to point out, the combination of brown and blue tones. Combining these colors in clothing is almost a symbol of being in the upper-middle class. (Picture 13, although not dealing with a plaid, combines beige and blue in another typically upper-middle-class manner.) In Picture 10, I have used the shirt to pick up the blue in the suit, and have used the paisley tie, which contains both brown and blue, to tie the look together.

Picture 11 is of another average businessman's plaid. I have included it so that I will be absolutely clear about exactly what an acceptable plaid business suit is. It is a plaid that can be seen, but one that is certainly not loud. The combination in Picture 11 also displays a very definite color lesson. If you choose any suit with elements of orange, rust or gold in it, you must pick a specific tie to compliment the suit. In this case, the only tie that is acceptable, even with the neutral white shirt, is one that picks up the orange in the suit. Any other color combinations of white and another color seem to clash.

My final plaid example, in Picture 12, is a very loud one. Such a jacket would not be acceptable in most business situations, but I chose it purposefully to indicate how a loud plaid may be calmed down. The jacket offers two very calming elements: one is the very thin yellow line that is picked up in the shirt; the other is the dark blue, which is picked up in the tie. Notice also that the tie is a knit, which again exerts a calming influence. A silk would be shiny and give more life. So texture is used to calm as well as to color.

Picture 13 shows one of the most useful year-round suits, the solid beige. As I have already indicated, it is combined with the blue shirt to indicate a very distinct upper-middle-class matching habit. The tie is used to show how a textured tie can pick up a textured shirt without picking up its color.

Picture 14 shows a blue jacket that could either be used as part of a suit, or as a sport jacket, simply by varying the tie. The solid shirt and the bright plaid tie give it a very sporty effect, one that is not at all serious and stands in marked contrast to its look in Picture 3. The jackets in both pictures are identical, yet the looks are miles apart, in both intent and effect.

Pictures 15 and 16 show the same traditional lightweight summer suit. In Picture 15, the suit is worn with a vest, a solid shirt and club tie, and as such would be proper summer attire at the most sedate business office. In Picture 16, the same suit is shown without the vest, with a plaid shirt and a bright bow tie. Here it is quickly transformed into a sport outfit. The two pictures indicate how shirts and ties can change the basic look of any suit, and how these versatile elements can make it wearable on many very different types of occasions.

In all of the pictures, none of the combinations is particularly clever, and although a few are nice, none is remarkably beautiful. These illustrations were designed to be used as teaching instruments, to illustrate principles. I could have just as easily chosen any of 500 possible combinations to make the same points.

I chose combinations that, by their nature, are not aesthetically tricky, because when you get up in the morning you are not likely to play games with tricky patterns and attempt to put them together. I also chose combinations that can be used by any businessman any day of his life, and I chose the types of suits that most men wear.

The one departure from the norm is the quality of the suits. All of those pictured here are from Bergdorf-Goodman in New York, and all retail for over $450. Although most men cannot afford such luxury in their wardrobes, I used these suits so you will be able to attempt to emulate as closely as possible the same richness of texture in the clothes you do buy.

Since the suit is the most important item in any clothing combination, it should always be bought first. Whenever you buy a suit, you should, as I have urged before, ask the tailor for a small piece of the material he takes off at the cuff. Staple that piece onto a business card. Beside it, write the date you bought the suit. If it's a solid suit, the piece should be about the size of a dime. If it's a pinstripe, make sure that your swatch contains all the colors of the pinstripe, and if it's a plaid, make sure that the swatch includes all the colors of the plaid. In time, you will have samples of your entire suit wardrobe in your wallet, so you can match them with specific shirts and ties whenever they are needed.

I suggest that you also write on the back of another business card a list of all the shirts you have at any given time. If you have followed the advice in this book, they will all be standard patterns and colors that will easily cross over for wear with more than one suit.

Armed with your suit swatches and shirt list, it should be a simple matter to buy ties to go with any feasible combination. You will also find it much easier to choose ties that can be worn with several combinations.

If you follow this system you will find that you are much better able to put your clothing together and will be able to do it less expensively than before because you are buying more practical garments. One of the great advantages of traditional colors, patterns and styles—in addition to their projecting the proper image of the successful man—is that they go further in a wardrobe and have a much longer wearable life because they are so adaptable.

As simple as my system is for any man who is willing to learn the correct styles, patterns and colors, I still have clients who want it easier. For some of them, I have set up their wardrobes as blue/gray systems with *every* shirt and tie matching *every* suit. In this way, whatever they put on works perfectly.

Others I have urged to observe two simple rules:

1. Never put two patterns next to each other.

2. Choosing only from the patterns of ties I have suggested in Chapter 4, buy ties that match or contrast with shirts and do not clash with suits.

Going along with only those two rules, a man can get up almost blind most mornings and go to work looking at least respectable, although I must admit that it limits one's wardrobe considerably.

DRESS FOR SUCCESS

Some readers who are both lazy and crafty will have by now discovered another way. Just take the pictures from the book and emulate the combinations with your own selections.

6

BUYING IT
CHEAP

If you follow the advice in this chapter, you will be able to dress as if you're buying your clothes on Fifth Avenue, even if you don't; you will be able to dress like a success, even if you aren't; and you will be able to save a great deal of money on the clothes you buy.

The first advice I always give clients is also the most obvious: Buy your clothing on sale. But don't just look for sales at random; plan ahead for them. There are two basic sales periods in the United States. In various parts of the country, the dates may change slightly, but basically fall–winter merchandise is on sale from approximately January 10 to February 5. Spring–summer merchandise usually goes on sale immediately after the July 4th weekend, and sales last through August.

During major sales the items offered are, as I'm sure you've noticed, of very mixed quality and varying desirability. So you must be carefully selective and I will give you guidelines about what to buy and when to buy.

The first priority is: Remember that you're going to buy at the times when sales are on. If you need a suit, wait until then if you possibly can. And when sales time comes, try to buy a few extra shirts, a few extra ties and an extra pair of shoes that you can stick in the closet for a while so you won't have to pay full price when you do need them. This does require planning, but it does pay off.

My second advice is to buy from factory outlets and discount stores, if these exist in your area. Obviously, men who live in large cities have a definite advantage, since there is an abundance of such stores to choose from. But here's a warning that goes with shopping anywhere that claims to offer substantial discounts. Quite often, such outlets offer no bargains at all. They sell shoddy goods; they mark them up by a far greater percentage than their discounts take prices down; and they do not mark flawed merchandise ("seconds") very well. I will tell you what to avoid as we go along, but remember: You must be careful.

Factory outlets and discount stores do have sales, too, at times when they must turn over stock. And if they really carry good merchandise, some incredible buys can be made at those times.

HOW TO COMPUTE ANY GARMENT'S TRUE COST

Before buying any article of clothing, make sure that you compute the true cost of the garment. I know very few men who do this, although it is very important. And in bad economic times, it is the only way to purchase. To compute the true cost of garments, let us assume that you see two raincoats on sale. One is marked $75.00 and the other $100.00. Both are waterproof, and should last approximately three years. But the $75.00 raincoat must be dry-cleaned; the $100.00 coat is made of a wash-and-wear fabric.

If you buy the $75.00 raincoat, you will probably get through the first year with only one cleaning. The second year will require two cleanings. To make the coat do through the third year will require three cleanings. If to dry-clean and waterproof it costs $15 each time, and you have had it cleaned five times, you have effectively doubled the price of the raincoat. On the other hand, the $100.00 raincoat, which you washed at home in your own machine, probably looked better when new and has cost only pennies more than its original price over a three-year period.

So it's wise to keep in mind that the cost of any article of clothing isn't only the price on the tag, but the *eventual* cost; and items that are "wash-and-wear" or "permanent press" frequently offer significant savings, even if their original purchase price is greater.

This is most evident in shirting. If you wish to save money, do not buy cotton shirts. A good cotton shirt costs more than polyester-and-cotton at the outset, and in the long run can cost three or four times as much. For example, you can today purchase a decent wash-and-wear shirt for $10.00. You can also purchase a fairly decent cotton shirt for $15.00, if you shop around a bit. If you wear the wash-and-wear shirt twenty times, washing it at home, your total expenditure for cleaning probably will come to around $1.00, plus the time of whoever does the minimum ironing it needs. The true cost of the shirt therefore adds up to $11.00.

Since very few people will iron a cotton shirt at home anymore, you will probably have to send it to a commercial laundry. If so, it probably won't last twenty times, but closer to ten, so you'll have to purchase two cotton shirts to get the same wear you get from the one wash-and-wear. This means that the true price of the shirt jumps from $15.00 to $30.00, plus the cost of twenty washings. Figured at 50 cents a wash, that pushes the cost of the cotton up to $40.00, as opposed to $11.00 for the wash-and-wear. I may be overestimating durability for some wash-and-wear shirts, but the example is valid.

You must also consider the expected lifespan of any garment. Three years ago, I purchased two car coats—one corduroy, one leather. The corduroy cost about $50.00, and the leather about $125.00. Three years later, the corduroy coat has cost me approximately another $25.00 in dry cleaning and is no longer usable. I therefore paid approximately $25.00 per year for my use of the corduroy coat. The leather coat has several years more wear left in it, and has cost me not a cent to clean. In the long run, the leather coat—which looked better and richer from the day of its purchase—will actually be cheaper than the corduroy coat.

The advice for economizing which I have given you so far has been available for years, and although it is rarely applied, it is hardly original. The element of sophistication that I can add to this advice is to have you purchase garments that look as if you had bought them in the most expensive stores and that they will last as long as the most expensive clothes available.

One of the great pluses of using my system of dress is that you will find that when you follow it, you will automatically begin buying better quality clothing, although you will pay no more for it. To accomplish this seemingly impossible miracle, you must learn to cross-shop—not just occasionally but as a way of life.

HOW TO MAKE CROSS-SHOPPING PAY OFF

Cross-shopping as a way of life means that at every opportunity, you go into stores that cater to various socioeconomic levels, particularly on the upper levels, and look at, feel and try on the merchandise. You must develop an interest not only in clothing, but in what clothing makes a man look successful: which shades or colors, which patterns, which fabrics and what kind of workmanship and tailoring. At first, cross-shopping will require a conscious effort, but after a while it will become a habit.

The real trick of cross-shopping, and the one that must be practiced right from the beginning, is to cross-shop for specific items. First, look at your wardrobe and decide what needs to be replaced. Then make a priority list for replacement. Let's assume that your dark gray suit is worn out, and you have neither a dark gray nor a dark blue. You might wish to replace the worn-out suit with a dark gray, a dark blue, or any other dark, conservative suit, in that order.

With your list of preferences, go to an inexpensive store. By inexpensive, I mean the store or stores that carry the lowest grade clothing that is acceptable to you. Look at the suits in that store. Then proceed to the most expensive store in your area, or several of them, and look at the suits there. Take a notebook with you and attempt to specify as many differences as you can between the look of the suits in the expensive store and the look in the inexpensive store.

First, differentiate between the looks of the materials. In the expensive store, suits might have a very soft look; in the inexpensive store, a very hard, shiny look.

Then look at specific workmanship characteristics. Are the buttons bone or plastic? Is the suit fully lined? Does it have an interior cigarette pocket? Does the pattern, if it has one, match where the material is sewn together? Is the fit good? Whatever differences you spot, jot them down.

Having now compared the best-looking suits with the cheapest that would be acceptable to you, go to the store that carries suits in a range of price you wish to spend, and see which suits most closely approximate the look of the expensive suits. The reason why you should always have a list of preferences is that in some cases you may come very close, while in others not at all. You may really want a gray suit, but the gray suit you can afford looks dramatically cheaper than its expensive counterpart. On the other hand, the dark blue comes closer. Buy the blue, or wait until you can find an acceptable gray in your price range.

Let's say you are looking for a blue shirt. Obviously, the very best blue dress shirt can be found in the expensive store. The color is pale; the fabric is soft; the buttons are bone; and the workmanship and fit are beautiful. But the same shade of blue can be found at a moderate price, and it can be found at a really cheap price. If you're really strapped for money, you should probably go for the cheapest, as long as it has the appropriate look. It won't fit as well; it won't last as long; it won't feel as good; but under a suit jacket, and with a decent tie, only an expert could tell.

Sometimes it is impossible to duplicate the pattern, texture, quality and look of expensive, tasteful garments at low prices. But only by cross-shopping will you be able to find out. When cross-shopping, you are determining availability at various price ranges. You will see where the limits are and where they are not, and you will be better able to determine how your money should be spent. You may be able to buy cheaper shirts, but pay more for ties. But always keep in mind that the least expensive item is not always truly the cheapest in total eventual cost; and, regardless of how much you spend, the point of your efforts is that you are trying to achieve *the look of success.*

HOW TO TELL GOOD LABELS FROM BAD LABELS

For the purposes of this book, stores selling clothing can be separated into a number of categories. First come those that stock only expensive, quality merchandise. In New York, examples that come to mind are Bergdorf Goodman, Saks Fifth Avenue, Brooks Brothers, F. R. Tripler, Paul Stuart, Lord and Taylor, Bloomingdale's, and B. Altman. While I might sometimes question the appropriateness of some of their clothing for a given individual in a given situation, I would never question the quality of their merchandise, nor their integrity in making good on occasional problems. But if you are looking for bargains, there is only one time to get them in these stores, at sale time.

In many of these stores, you will find a variety of labels, and the significance of these labels is very important. First, you will find designer labels, and regardless of the quality of the garments, when you buy designer-labeled apparel, you are paying something for the famous name and you really don't get your money's worth. If you're buying at a top level store, you have their own quality guarantee anyway. In addition, the greatest percentage of designer clothing is in the high-fashion category, and, as I've emphasized elsewhere in this book, inappropriate for most American men.

Invariably, you will also find the store's own label, and by-and-large it offers the best quality-for-dollar buy. The store labels of reputable stores are generally excellent, and very often are applied to merchandise identical to that of manufacturers with famous designer goods.

The third label is a combination, "So-and-so Clothing Made Specifically For (and then the name of the store)." This labeling is also a good indicator of quality in expensive stores. It means that the store's buyer believes that the brand is good enough to put the store label on it, and that the manufacturer's name and reputation are significant enough to warrant mentioning. It may also mean that the buyer has the right of rejection to a certain percentage of that manufacturer's goods as a further guarantee of quality control. This means that, to some extent, the garments have been pre-selected for you, and also that you may well find the rejected goods elsewhere at significant savings.

Next in the categories of stores selling clothing comes that group of large department stores whose merchandise and prices are aimed directly at the middle class. Their quality ranges from excellent to moderate, and they also have a labeling system that offers solid value indicators to the man who isn't an expert on clothing.

Some of these stores carry clothes with designer labels; again, they are to be avoided by the cost conscious. Most of the big department stores also sell their own store label, and this is an indication that the item so labeled is an excellent quality-for-dollar buy, as is the combination label featuring the name of the manufacturer as well as the store.

Department stores usually also carry two additional labels. The first is that of well-known, mass distribution manufacturers whose merchandise is as good as their present reputation. The other is what I call the "diddledy-diddledy-boom label." This is basically a made-up name owned by the store. It is applied to merchandise with which the store doesn't want its own name associated, but which it believes offers good dollar-value for the price. This type of label usually appears on the cheapest line of merchandise that the store carries.

If you must buy really inexpensively, neither the expensive, first-class stores nor the large department stores are the best places for you. But they do offer many advantages: variety, quality control, customer services, generous merchandise return policies, excellent (and free) tailoring services.

If you are difficult to fit, the cost of tailoring is a very important consideration when you buy suits and estimate their true cost. If you are an exceptionally difficult fit, it is not inconceivable that tailoring could run $25.00 to $50.00 for a suit, and your money is much better spent on a higher quality suit to begin with than on tailoring.

Whatever the good points of expensive shops or department stores, it is a fact that the vast majority of men in this country cannot afford to buy clothes in these types of stores. For these men, there are three other kinds of stores that offer decent merchandise in a lower price range.

First are the chain stores, the large chains that have stores throughout the country and put their own name on virtually all of their merchandise, or have made-up names for categories of their merchandise that are almost synonymous with the store name.

Their clothing is relatively inexpensive, and is worth just about what you pay for it. Their sales do not offer great bargains, but are generally reliable. The only suggestions I have about shopping in such chains is to read the other chapters in this book very carefully, to know what you are looking for and need, and to do considerable cross-shopping before ever buying anything. Regardless of what you can spend, you are still trying to buy clothes that give off a distinct image.

HOW TO WATCH YOUR STEP IN DISCOUNT STORES

Next, consider the discount stores. These generally offer the the most inexpensive acceptable clothes, but these outlets also must be approached with considerable care and some knowledge of fabrics and workmanship if you want to look successful. You must check for quality and for value.

Discount stores fall into only two categories: honest and dishonest. Honest discount stores can sell at their low prices because they buy merchandise that is sacrificed elsewhere. They buy manufacturer's overruns; and they take on distress merchandise from stores that are in financial trouble. Discount stores also bring in a regular supply of their own merchandise, and this is their weakest point. Their own lines are not quality goods sold at a discount, but cheap goods being sold inexpensively. So before you buy at any discount store, you should familiarize yourself with the labels that are consistently offered there and nowhere else. These are the labels owned by the discount store, and you should avoid clothing so marked, since it represents your worst buy.

You must also be extra aware of current fashion when you shop in discount stores, because they carry many articles that are so far removed from prevailing styles as to be just about worthless in trying to build your image. But sometimes you can find items that are dated but can be corrected, if you pick and choose with care and know a good tailor.

I recently bought a designer-labeled suit in a discount house for $21.00. It had retailed for $100.00, but it had very wide bell-bottom pants, so large that no one should wear them. My tailor cut down the pants for $14.00. I now have an excellent, beautiful summer suit—and it cost me only $35.00. Please note that I do not apologize for picking up a bargain; I brag about it!

Many discount stores also carry mass-distribution brand-name merchandise at a discount rate, and this offers the best buys on a consistent basis. There is no better guarantee of quality, and first-line merchandise and seconds are usually carefully marked. Some discount stores cut out the brand names, and that is also usually a good indicator of quality. True, you will find some crooked merchants cutting labels out of shoddy goods, and selling them as brands that they are not, but if you do your cross-shopping, you will be able to quickly detect these obvious frauds.

Dishonest discount stores frequently identify their true colors without your having to do any detective work. The least reputable places have one characteristic in common, and that's the high-pressure salesmen. Almost invariably, they try to push certain goods on you. If they're pushing, they probably have a good reason, since the honest discounter has little trouble moving his merchandise. Salesmen who push are working on a commission basis, and their advice is going to be in their best interest rather than yours.

Don't for one second believe that the day of the huckster in clothing stores is over. On a Saturday afternoon about a year ago, I went shopping the discount stores for a raincoat. After going to several stores where they very frankly told me they didn't have what I wanted, I arrived at the third store and asked for my size, which happens to be 42 Long. One salesmen said they didn't have it, but immediately another fellow jumped up and said, "Oh yes, we have it!"

He quickly took a coat down from a rack and helped me on with it without giving me a chance to look at it at all. He then pulled up some of the material in the back with his hand so that from the front the coat looked as if it fit. It was actually a 46 Regular. I took it off, and my wife and I began laughing. The salesman, who thought that he just had suckered me, was busy putting the coat in a box and wrapping it, and it took him a while to realize that we were laughing at him.

Although this scene looked like something out of a 1920s cartoon, such practices are still going on. And although it seems absurd, that salesman must have gotten away with such shenanigans before. So the phrase *caveat emptor* very definitely prevails when you are buying clothing at a discount.

Another type of discount store is the so-called "manufacturer's outlet." These fall into three categories. First is the manufacturer's outlet that isn't. This type of store does not carry standard lines and stock but merely uses the designation as a come-on. Their merchandise is purchased from odd lots, damaged goods or seconds. Another practice is to purchase goods, mark them up 200 percent, and then discount them 50 percent.

The second type of manufacturer's outlet, which is quite legitimate and which offers excellent buys if you hit them at the right time, is the factory outlet that is actually next to the factory and owned by the manufacturer. These outlets sell their own overproduction, seconds, dated goods and odd lots.

If you don't know what odd lots are, I should explain; if you do, bear with me for a moment. You buy shirts one at a time, but retailers naturally do not. They buy an entire line and must have all sizes available. Obviously, the store must have more of the most popular sizes—15½–33 for example—than of others. At some point during the season, the manufacturer will be left with some patterns or colors or materials of shirts in which he doesn't have every size. If he chooses not to replenish his stock with the missing sizes, or if he can no longer obtain that specific material, he disposes of his remainders as odd lots. The man who wears unusual sizes can consequently do very well in factory outlets.

The one major flaw of shopping in such factory outlets is that they do not mark their seconds very well. Many put out seconds and overproduction and odd lots and mix them all together so that you can buy two shirts at the same counter at the same price and one will be in terrific shape and the other will have a bad flaw. Until you unwrap the shirt, you never know. The practice verges on being dishonest, but it is being done right along. So examine all merchandise carefully before paying for it. Although the discounts in factory outlets are substantial— usually 50 percent or more—return policies are practically nonexistent.

The other legitimate type of factory outlet is independently owned, but sells a number of lesser-known brands. These brands are possibly just as good as those of the major manufacturers, maybe even better, but the stocks in these stores consist not only of overproduction and odd lots but also seconds and dated goods.

This type of factory outlet is a tricky place to shop, and for a very simple reason. During good times, a manufacturer can sell almost all his goods to regular retail stores at the highest possible profits. If he owns his own factory outlet, the manufacturer can keep it supplied from regular stock, and still make a maximum profit. But in such times, he's only going to supply the independent outlet when it suits him.

When times are tough and manufacturers are having a hard time moving their merchandise, independent outlets tend to stock good merchandise at excellent buys. But in good times, to keep the independent outlet operating, the owner will have to purchase goods that are frequently of secondary quality and higher costs, and sell such goods as if they are being substantially discounted. So the outlet at times delivers exactly what it says it delivers, but at times it doesn't. Therefore, you can't go into one of these places and buy blindly. You must look very carefully, and you must look for labels you recognize; they are very important.

In New York one weekend, I came across items of clothing, discounted by 50 percent or more, of the following brands: Aquascutum, Arrow, Stanley Blacker, Pierre Cardin, Clubman, Countess Mara, Hammonton Park, His, Hush Puppies, Duofold, English Daks, Eagle, Jantzen, Lee, Johnston & Murphy, London Fog, MacGregor, Monte Cristo, Mr. Pants, Oleg Cassini, Palm Beach, Phoenix, Prince Ferrara, Sero, Schiaperelli and Sussex. In addition, there were many more good buys on garments with the labels removed, or carrying a store label known to New Yorkers. And I saw the labels of seven stores that sell only high quality goods.

On that one weekend, if you had previously cross-shopped with any care at all, you could have bought half a dozen suits, several brands of shirts, ties, raincoats and shoes at half price or less, and would have wound up with the same items that at the same time were being sold in elegant Fifth Avenue stores at regular price.

When one of my most successful clients availed himself of my services, he said he knew absolutely nothing about brands or labels or store names. So he developed his own system. Every time he went into a good store, he would write in an alphabetized pocket address book the brand name or label, the retail price, and brief description of any garment he bought. After about four months, he had also compiled a listing for every article of clothing he might still need, as well as those brands that were acceptable in quality and appearance. When he went to the discount houses, he simply whipped out his little book, and bought or didn't buy according to what he found.

He figured that he was saving 40 percent on his clothing bill as a direct result of this record-keeping, and he was able to wear exactly the same clothing he would have purchased in the more expensive stores. So the notebook method is a good one.

Discount stores and factory outlets are fine for the man who lives in a city large enough to support them, but what about the man who lives in a small town or in a city that is not a good town for buying clothing? He can shop at sales time, but then he is usually faced with a relatively limited selection.

GET A "FREE" TRIP TO NEW YORK

Many of my out-of-town clients have discovered that if they come to New York in late January or early February, they can purchase their clothes so economically that the trip is paid for by their savings. Among my clients, this custom started some years ago with eight midwestern doctors. It has now grown to the point that there are probably 300 to 400 Molloy clients (and their wives) in New York during January, and their annual clothes-buying trips have become organized vacations.

I do not recommend that everyone in similar circumstances

necessarily take this type of vacation. I do suggest that any man who finds himself in a large city try to take advantage of whatever clothing bargains may be waiting there. Whenever I'm in a new town, I always ask if the town has any famous factory outlets. Quite often local companies are proud to show off their goods, and a shopper can do very well by being a bit inquisitive and aggressive.

Saving money on clothing can also be accomplished just by buying less clothing. You can do this without sacrifices because conservative, traditional styles will go much further in your wardrobe than nontraditional styles.

The careful buyer should also consider multifunctional items. I haven't bought a solid blue or camel hair sport jacket in years, but I always have one of each. Every two or three years I buy a suit that gives me those types of jacket. Usually the suits are more expensive than what I would normally pay because I want a very rich look in the jacket; but it performs a dual function, and so the money averages out. The first year I use it only as a suit. The second year I wear the jacket with contrasting pants, as well as with the suit pants.

You should also consider buying suits that are sold with an extra pair of pants. This is an excellent idea that frequently prolongs the life of a suit even though the garments are not normally of the best quality or appropriate patterns and colors. I have one friend who shops at Brooks Brothers but never buys a suit unless they tailor-make him a matching second pair of pants. This runs into money, but the true cost is not forbidding in the long run.

The man who is truly eager to save money on his clothing should always have two lists with him. The first is a list of items he is going to need in the next year. Purchasing any further ahead can be a waste, since you can change weight or move to another section of the country where needs are different.

The second list should consist of items you can use at any time. For example, anytime I see a good solid blue or solid maroon silk tie on sale, I buy it, since I know I will need it at some point in the future. Right now I have half a dozen unworn maroon silk ties, but I paid half price or less for them, and I know I'll have one when I need it, and I won't have to pay full price.

My next recommendation for saving money and improving the quality of your clothing is comparison living. Comparison *shopping* is difficult. Unless you're an expert, it's often very hard to discern quality differences when you hold up two shirts in a store. Although I owned a shirt outlet for three years and my business is clothes, I can still be fooled about the quality of one versus another. But I have developed a second system of comparison living, and many of my clients and I use it.

Whenever we find a brand we like—whether it's a make of suits, shirts, ties or shoes—we keep a running record of how many wearings that brand gives us. We compare this with different brands in a comparative price range and are very often surprised to find that some of the brands we've experienced in the past as being very good are becoming shoddy.

Two developments are characteristic of inflationary times. Some well-known manufacturers maintain their quality and raise prices at the risk of losing some customers. Others cut down on quality to maintain prices and keep customers. You cannot readily notice these quality differences in the store, but you can pinpoint them after a number of wearings of a garment. That's comparative living, a continuing reevaluation of quality and price, and the only way for the intelligent clothes buyer to stay ahead of the game in hard times.

HOW TO SPOT IMPORTED BARGAINS

Another factor that many bargain-conscious men also tend to overlook is the comparative cost and quality between imported and domestic goods. Some countries-of-origin produce goods of consistent high quality at fairly reasonable prices, usually thanks to low-cost, well-skilled labor.

Although any buyer should always be wary of generalities,

I can offer some hints. Imported shoes from Brazil presently seem to be the best buy. There are fine shoes from Italy, beautiful ones from Greece, and good ones from England, Ireland, France and Germany, but the best buys are from Brazil.

For suits, there are three levels of imports. At the lowest, the best buys are from the large chain stores that are more and more obtaining their goods from the Orient. At the moderate level, American-made suits are the best value. At the very expensive price level, European suits offer the best quality-for-dollar-spent ratio.

In shirts, the best polyester-and-cotton blends are undoubtedly American. With good cotton shirts, the point of origin doesn't seem to matter.

The best moderate-priced silk ties are Italian; the best polyester, American. Although there are no tremendous breakthroughs in this field, there are some good ties coming from the Orient, along with a lot of junk.

American-made socks, underwear and outerwear offer the best values.

Good buys on sweaters are available from Mexico and Yugoslavia (of the Iron Curtain countries, Yugoslavia is the only one that makes and exports fashionable items to any extent).

Gold and silver cuff links are generally very good buys when you can pick them up in many Caribbean islands and in Mexico. And although the international monetary fluctuations have made foreign shopping much more expensive in recent years, there are still some good buys for the careful tourist in Europe.

A SYSTEM TO SAVE $17,000

A few years ago, I asked seven new clients to keep a record of how much time they spent looking for clothing over a three-year period, and to make up an approximate cost analysis of how much they saved. Four of the men are lawyers; the other three work in sales-related fields. All are reasonably affluent and good dressers.

In the first year, when each of them was spending quite a bit of time on his learning process, they estimated that they were only saving the equivalent of about $1.00 per hour spent in shopping. At the end of the second year, they were saving about $1.50 to $2.00 an hour, depending on the man. And at the end of the third year, they were saving from $4.00 to $6.00 an hour —and having a very good time doing it.

After the third year, these seven men estimated that they saved $300 to $350 a year on their clothing (with inflation, these figures would now be closer to $500). This is a rather substantial figure, and is largely due to their living in New York with all its resources. But if we take that figure and do a bit of simple multiplication, we come to the astounding conclusion that in the buyer's lifetime of fifty years, he can save in excess of $17,000 —and that's just as good as $17,000 of tax-free income.

After everything is said and done, you must spend either time or money to dress successfully. If you have the money and are willing to spend it on clothes, then all you need are the general and basic instructions found elsewhere in this book. But if you don't have the money, or want to hold on to as much as you can, you can still dress just as successfully if you are willing to spend the time, and if you know and adhere to the rules of American dress.

7.

HOW TO USE CLOTHES TO SELL YOURSELF

The most common form of motivation is the desire to make a sale. Selling is a process that affects everybody and in which all of us engage at many times in our lives, whether we are selling products, services, concepts or ourselves. The basic, most important point of this entire book is that any man, whether in business or in his social life (and aren't the two often inseparable?), can "sell" himself far more successfully through the adroit manipulation of his clothing than he can by any other means.

To the great majority of men a sale is anything but a casual, periodic occurrence. It is absolutely the most dominant force in their lives and is responsible on a crucial day-to-day basis for their businesses, their jobs, their economic well-being, their very existence and subsistence. It is for these men that this chapter is written.*

To cover every aspect of clothing—and of motivating your fellow man—that my research has shown to be important would

---

*Although this chapter is being specifically written for men whose lives are directly or indirectly concerned with sales, the information is equally valid and practical for any man.

require volumes, and would be of limited interest to the general reader for whom this book is written. So I will confine myself to the most crucial details.

All sales, all motivation, is a three-factor process—a seller, a buyer and a product. Starting with the seller and the buyer, the controllable elements of any sale can be broken down into simple categories. They are:

The appearance of the seller and the appearance of the buyer.

The company orientation of the seller and the company orientation of the buyer.

The age of the seller and the age of the buyer.

The socioeconomic level of the seller and the socioeconomic level of the buyer at the time of the sale.

The socioeconomic background of the seller and the socioeconomic background of the buyer.

The race of the seller and the race of the buyer.

The geographical location from which the seller comes and the geographical location from which the buyer comes.

The training, or industrial orientation, of the seller and the training, or industrial orientation, of the buyer.

The sex of the seller and the sex of the buyer.

All of these elements have been statistically proven to exercise an effect on whether people like you, believe you—and buy from you.

I know that a great many salesmen will scoff when they read this, particularly those who are successful. In order to be good, salesmen must have enormous egos to overcome their constant defeat, because all selling is a percentage of hit and miss. And all successful salesmen, as part of their own ego-propping, come to believe that they and their golden voices are responsible for sales. The mere idea that any other factors play any role whatsoever will come to them as a somewhat ego-deflating defeat.

I ask these men to hold their criticism for a while. By the time they have reached the middle of this chapter, if they're really good salesmen, they will begin to see that sales and nonverbal communicants are twin brothers in the business of persuasion. If they are really superb at their jobs, they will also begin to see that they have been using clothing and other nonverbal communicants for years.

For other salesmen, those who have been at it for a while but are largely unsuccessful, I suggest the strictest attention. Whenever I speak before a sales force, or work with a sales force, I can virtually guarantee that I can substantially help half of the salesmen who are failures, and this group makes up about two-thirds of most sales forces. I can help them because their failure is based on the fact that they consistently project the wrong nonverbal communications.

Their sales are lost, not when they open their mouths, but before they open them. They do not lose sales because they give the wrong sales pitch; they would lose no matter what sales pitch they come up with. They lose because their appearances convey that they are not likeable, they are not honest, they are not trustworthy, they are not even sincere. If these men will read carefully, I will show the largest percentage of them how to appear likeable, honest, credible and sincere. I will show them how to sell.

NEVER UNDERESTIMATE THE POWER OF A HAIRCUT

Several years ago, I was lecturing a group of young lawyers on selling themselves in the courtroom. One of the desirable influences that I mentioned was very moderate hair, and four or five of the young men said, "Well, we're certainly okay on that score, because that definitely describes our haircuts."

I didn't really think so, but instead of contradicting them outright I decided to put their haircuts to a test. We had pictures drawn of each of the young men; more precisely, we had pictures drawn of their haircuts on blank faces. Each of the young lawyers took a picture of one of the other young lawyer's haircut to work with him and queried the senior partners in his firm about the appropriateness of the haircut for court. The senior

16 WAYS TO LOOK RIGHT
WITHOUT EFFORT

1

solid suit
striped shirt
solid tie

2

solid suit
plaid shirt
solid tie

3

solid suit
white shirt
Ivy League tie

4

solid suit
white shirt
Ivy League tie

5
striped suit
striped shirt
plaid-type tie

6
striped suit
white shirt
polka dot tie

7
striped suit
solid shirt
rep tie

8
striped suit
solid shirt
solid tie

9
plaid suit
solid shirt
plaid tie

10
plaid suit
solid shirt
paisley tie

11
plaid suit
solid shirt
Ivy League tie

12
plaid jacket
solid shirt
solid tie

13
beige suit
textured shirt
textured tie

14
blue jacket
solid shirt
plaid tie

15
summer striped suit
vest—solid shirt
club tie

16
summer striped suit
plaid shirt
bow tie

partners, who were roughly equivalent in age and temperament to the judges before whom the young lawyers worked, all made negative comments about every haircut, judging them to be too long, too effeminate, too kookie, etc.

The fact is that older men, in positions of responsibility and authority, expect everyone they meet to have hair that is acceptable to them. What you think of your hair length and style is totally irrelevant; what society thinks is largely irrelevant, too. What matters are the opinions of those men who are in positions to make judgments about you that will either help or hurt. This varies from man to man and locality to locality. There are no general rules I can offer, but it is a matter of importance, and you must learn for yourself what haircut is acceptable in your specific circumstances and adopt it.

I am frequently asked if there are any traits common to all successful executives. There most definitely are; they always have their hair combed and their shoes shined. And they expect the same of other men, particularly subordinates. If your hair is disheveled, even if it is short, it triggers very strong negative reactions from other men. Keep it neat, and if you have hair that happens to grow in every possible direction except the right one, then you had better find something that will keep it down, or a barber who can give you a cut that minimizes the problem.

I hate to tell you this, but there is also a direct correlation between the shape of a man's face and his chances of success. The most successful face is masculine and elongated, neither too heavy nor too thin, without prominent features. In short, the perfect WASP face. Slight faces are judged as being effeminate and round faces as being ineffectual. That's the bad news. The good news is that hair can help, if you can find someone to cut it who knows what he is doing.

I have ears that stick out, and look very silly in a short haircut that makes my ears look even more prominent than they are. Hair that slightly covers my ears masks the problem entirely. Men with dark hair look stronger than men with light hair, and a small man with dark hair can make himself seem more powerful by picking up the darkness of the hair in the darkness of his suit, and by letting his hair be slightly longer than average. If a man has blond or red hair, it is a bad mistake to pick up either color in his clothing.

Older men can look much younger by affecting younger hair styles and by coloring out the gray if looking younger is a business necessity. Usually it is the opposite, and I have occasionally advised young men who are already in positions of authority and responsibility to make themselves look more distinguished by slightly, very slightly, graying their sideburns.

Changing one's hair style or hair color to make one more effective is definitely not effeminate and should not be considered as such. It is positively Machiavellian—and it works.

Blacks in the business world should never wear Afro haircuts. Men who do are less highly thought of by both whites and blacks, and are much less likely to succeed in any endeavor. (See Chapter 8, "Some Advice for Minorities.")

Most men should not wear facial hair of any kind. The response to facial hair is almost always negative in corporate situations, and the only men who should wear it are those men who must compensate for some other weakness in their appearance or personality. A beard and/or a mustache can make a man more powerful and more masculine-looking. If a man has no chin, a beard can mask that oversight of nature. If a man looks very young, a mustache or beard can speed up the ageing process.

If a man does decide he needs a mustache, it should always be moderate—no handlebars, no pencil stripes. Beards should be full, and goatees should be avoided at all costs. People do not trust or believe men in goatees; perhaps it's the devil image— I don't know.

Very heavy beards (or long ones) look old-fashioned and out of date. All facial hair should be kept well trimmed and well shaped. If you are in any business that requires business lunches, for heaven's sake, make sure that you constantly keep your mustache and/or beard clean of food particles.

HOW TO USE EYEGLASSES

Any man who must wear glasses must also recognize that they are significant factors in his total look, either contributing to it or detracting from it. The man who has good features or the man for whom any glasses are a negative influence should definitely consider contact lenses.

Wire frames are considered chic and up-to-date. They have been around long enough so that anyone can now wear them, but they always look much better on younger men. Heavy plastic or horn rims are more traditional, powerful and make a man look older.

If glasses must be chosen to offset or enhance a particular facial characteristic, then trial and error is the only real way of determining what is best for any individual.

Men with heavy lower jaws and cheeks should probably wear heavier glasses, and men with lighter, thinner lower faces should probably wear lighter glasses. In both cases, the use of the glasses can help pull the upper and lower face together into a compatible unit. Very young men who must establish their authority may find that picking up their hair color in the color of their frames is effective.

HOW TO CAMOUFLAGE LIABILITIES OF PHYSICAL APPEARANCE

The most important element in establishing a man's authority is his physical size, and most men obviously fall into three size categories—large, average and small. Unfortunately, these dimensions cannot be broken down into specific combinations of feet, inches and pounds, because size, as it applies to what clothing should be worn, is relative. But most men should have no problem in classifying themselves correctly if they carefully compare themselves to the men with whom they have the most contact.

Large men, or men who have a forbidding or gruff appearance, have an advantage and a disadvantage. The advantage is that they tend to be extremely authoritative. When they speak with authority, people generally tend to believe them, even when they are only extolling the relative values of a so-so automobile or the function of an average computer. They are more likely to be believed about technical matters than average-size men or short men. Their tremendous disadvantage, particularly if they are very large or have a very hard look, is that they frighten people.

In one of my most interesting sales experiments, I selected six purchasing agents of very short stature and videotaped them in their daily job encounters over a three-week period. They believed I was filming the salesmen that visited them and consequently paid little attention to the camera. I discovered that when large salesmen came into their offices, the purchasing agents were often verbally rude. They were abrupt and frequently chased the salesmen from the offices. The purchasing agents seemed to be in complete command. However, when we played the film back without the sound, the purchasing agents looked as if they were defending themselves from attackers.

After some in depth questioning, I came to the conclusion that when a man who is selling is much larger than the man who is buying, he can and often does frighten the buyer, and it is essential that he do everything in his power not to scare his client. A frightened man will immediately turn you off. He will escape from you, even if it means throwing you out of the office.

I told this to a sales manager once, and he said, "You've got to be crazy. My best salesman is an ex-football player; the man's a monster. He sells twice as much as any other man in the place, and he doesn't obey your rules of dress."

I said I'd like to speak with the man, and the sales manager had him come in. While most football players are stereotyped as big, dumb and insensitive, this man was anything but. When I explained my position to him, he said, "Yes, I agree."

His boss then said, "Well, how can that be? If you scare people, how the hell do you get them to buy so much?"

The salesmen said, "I'll show you," and he got up, walked to the door and did a stage fall. His boss asked, "Well, what's that?" And the man replied, "When I walk into a man's office and I catch that glimmer of fear in his eyes—which I've become very sensitive to lately—I simply fall down. I pretend I've hurt my leg and have him help me. That puts *me* in the defensive position and enables me to make the sale."

I told that story at a sales meeting I was addressing about six months later, and afterward I was approached by another ex-football player who told me his approach. He said, "When I walk into an office, I look for that same sense of fear. I didn't really know what it was, but I thought I was being too aggressive. Whenever I see a man on the defensive, I simply drop my papers all over the floor and start groveling for them. Often the man comes around and helps me, and when he does, I usually have a sure sale."

These two very large men overcame their problems of frightening their clients in two different ways. The third way is to do it with clothing.

The large man should avoid all dark, high-authority suits, should never wear pinstripes and never wear vests. He should wear very soft colors and textures: medium-range soft gray suits, beige suits and very light suits in summer. A combination I have found particularly effective is a medium-range gray suit with medium-range blue shirt and a gray and blue tie.

The large man should avoid strong color contrasts and any articles of clothing that call attention to him. He is the only man, in terms of size, who should wear nonauthoritative ties, and either wear those outside the recommended ones in Chapter 4, or, if he wishes to remain within that group, stick with reps and solids only.

The large man should only wear very light shoes, and should avoid the heavier shoes, such as wingtips, that are normally a staple of any businessman's attire.

The primary mistake made by most large men is not that they dress too authoritatively; somehow they have an instinct that protects them against that mistake. What they do, though, is to go into one of the so-called Big Man's shops that are now fairly widespread around the country, and take the advice of the clerks in these stores. They show the large man loud, bright, gaudy garments and tell him how wonderful it is that he can now wear such clothing which in the past was not manufactured in large sizes. Well, if he couldn't wear them before, he shouldn't wear them now. Although they are by no means authoritative clothes, they are not right for selling, no matter what your size is.

Along with the very large man, the man with a gruff appearance and the man with a very deep voice (or a combination of all three), I would include among problem salesmen: the very short man, the man with the high-pitched voice, the man who is very thin and the man who has a round, cherubic, ineffective-looking face. These men have two problems—an authority problem and a problem of presence. The authority problem is that if they are sitting in a one-to-one business situation, they will not be believed as readily as a larger man. If they are in a group situation, their presence is not noticed and they are less effective. So they must fight both problems at once.

HERE'S HELP FOR THE SMALL MAN

The authority problem is easily solved by wearing high-authority clothing: pinstripe suits, pinstripe shirts, Ivy League ties, vests. If, in addition to being very small, the man is young, he should only wear ties that are very expensive, $20.00 and above. I realize that this is a very expensive suggestion and the advice contradicts what I said in the tie chapter, but this man must wear ties that obviously would not be available to a boy. One of the major problems with small men who are very young is that people still are tempted to address them as, "Hey, kid." To overcome this, they should only wear super-adult garments, the most obvious being the expensive tie.

The best shirt for the small man is the solid white; the best shoes are traditional wingtips; the best coats are heavy and luxurious, such as camel hair. They should wear only rich looking attire, and they should be neat to the point of being precise.

Color contrast is very important for these men, and it is easily attainable with a dark suit, white shirt and dark tie. They should make sure that the contrast is equally pronounced in their sport clothes, particularly between any two items worn above the belt. If a golf jacket and a golf shirt are both in the same shade range, they will make the small man look even smaller.

Small men should wear attention-getting devices, including even those that I do not recommended for anyone else. A handkerchief showing from the breast pocket of the suit jacket, a diamond stickpin in this age when no one else wears them— these items have worked well for men I know. The best device of all that I've found is a unique watch that is immediately identifiable as quite expensive. Those made from gold coins or quartz crystal digitals seem to work particularly well in bestowing an aura of substance on a short man.

If a short or thin man wears glasses, the frames should be fairly heavy to add significance to his face. He should carry the most masculine-looking attaché case he can afford. And under no circumstances should he carry an umbrella. Never. I don't give a damn if it's raining cats and dogs; wear a raincoat and get wet. Do not carry an umbrella! It's a death knell for the small man. It turns him into a Wally Cox pipsqueak figure, ineffective but nice. And that is no image for a salesman of anything. Not for a successful salesman, anyway.

Men who are of slightly above-average weight and men who are slightly below average in size have fewer problems with their appearance than do very large and very short men, but they can also improve their effectiveness through their clothing. Men who are slightly above average can wear authoritative suits, but should avoid the most authoritative ties. The easiest, simplest way of diminishing authority and fright caused by size is by wearing one bright item of attire, and the tie is the best element to use.

The slightly above-average man should know that his size is

an advantage in business, giving him a definite psychological edge over smaller men, and he should use his size to his advantage. If his superior is smaller than he is, he should wear soft or light-colored suits and avoid strong contrasts when dealing with him, so as not to antagonize or threaten him.

The man who is slightly below average height may keep his wardrobe in the same range as the average man (using the colors and patterns recommended in previous chapters), but he should be careful not to let his wardrobe be too drab, and he should stay away from sporty ties (the paisley) and wear only serious ties (Ivy League and polka-dot). If the slightly below average man is working with men who are exceptionally large, and this does happen on occasion, then he should adapt the dress code of the very short man and become extremely precise in his appearance, since size is definitely a relative matter and one must manipulate his authority quotient accordingly.

WHAT IF YOU'RE JUST BUILT "SLOPPY"?

Some of us have a problem that, while related to size, is somewhat more difficult to define. It is simply that we are built in a sloppy way. Certain men look neat no matter what they do, and others will *never* look neat no matter what they do. If you are one of the unfortunates in the latter category, as I am, you must make a conscious effort always to have your hair combed, to have a very high shine on your shoes, to make sure that your shirt is never disheveled and that your tie knot is always at your collar.

The best way of accomplishing all this is to set up a daily routine when you check these tell-tale signs on a regular basis. The disheveled man never goes anywhere, except out for coffee. When he tries to sell, he cannot successfully sell any item that people consider serious. If you are a sales manager, never hire a disheveled salesman; if you have one, make him neaten up or move out.

How to Use Clothes to Sell Yourself

Geography can hurt you. If you live in a sophisticated area and sell in a less sophisticated area, you must never wear items of apparel that are markedly more sophisticated than what's worn by the people to whom you are selling. If you go from New York to Kansas City, if you go from Kansas City to a town 200 miles out on the prairie, if you go from Chicago to southern Illinois, you must never look as if you are better than the people you are selling to, because they will object to you, and may not buy from you.

Examples of such an elitest display would be the Ivy League tie worn by the Northeasterner when he sells in the South, the newest designer suit from Kansas City that is not yet available in Pratt, Kansas, the Gucci shoe worn by the "smartass" New Yorker when he's selling in San Antonio.

The reverse of this rule is equally important not to violate. If you come from a small town and are selling in a more sophisticated area, you must be sure not to wear items that will mark you as a rube. It is quite common to see Southerners in New York wearing very bright colors and patterns. In Atlanta, this is perfectly acceptable, but it isn't in the New York business community, and it marks the Southerners as out-of-towners and hayseeds.

Many Texas salesmen wear their ten-gallon hats and string ties when they go selling in the Northwest. I once pointed this out to a group of Texas salesmen as being inappropriate. They said, "Well, they can go to hell if they don't like our clothes." I said, "Yes, that's fine, but they'll go more times than not without buying your product." They didn't care for that thought.

The most conservative business areas in the United States, as regards clothing, are Wall Street, Washington, D.C. and Boston. The corporate headquarters of any major firm, no matter where it is located, fits into the same category. In any of these places, if you show up to sell, you must be dressed in the standard Northeast establishment attire if you are to be as effective as possible. The men who wear this attire run the country, make no mistake about it, and if they are to deal with you as an equal, they expect you to follow suit.

The most acceptable clothing for dealing with these men are dark and medium-range gray suits, dark and medium-range blue suits, with or without pinstripes. White or blue solid shirts are preferable, as are all conservative ties, with the exception of the Ivy League. You should avoid the Ivy League tie unless you are sure that the people you're going to be dealing with are also wearing it.

When selling in the remainder of the country, it is best to avoid the pinstripe suit and Ivy League tie. Solid blue and solid gray suits are acceptable almost anywhere and are generally the safest. The plaid suit is perfectly acceptable business attire outside of the most conservative areas, provided it is a subtle plaid and not one of the plaids you see on farmboys from Georgia, grocery clerks from Brooklyn and almost anyone from Philadelphia.

I mention Philadelphia, not to pick on its upright residents but to point out that Philadelphia is subject to a very unusual set of clothing rules; indeed, they are unique to that city. Even though Philadelphia is noted for conservatism, its bankers dress even more gaudily than bankers from the West Coast, which is noted for gaudy attire. I can offer no reasons for this paradox, but it does demonstrate the importance of your taking notice of clothing codes whenever you're in an unfamiliar area, and adjusting your own wardrobe accordingly.

WHAT'S BEST IN THE SOUTH

Some areas of the country do have specific dress rules, and over the years I have compiled a list of do's and don'ts for selling in these areas.

First, the South. If you are not a Southerner but you're selling in the South, never wear a polka-dot tie. If you are a

Southerner, it is acceptable. Don't wear dark pinstripe suits when selling in the South; medium-range solid blues and grays are better than dark blues or grays. Outside of Atlanta and Dallas, you should avoid dressing in the latest fashion. In Atlanta, in most industries, you should dress only in the latest fashions. In most of the South, the white shirt is still the safest shirt. Lavender and pink shirts elicit a strong negative reaction.

You will cut down your credibility in the South if you are wearing an Ivy League tie or any type of fancy footwear. In the South, if you are an outsider, do not wear any attire that is peculiar to the area: cowboy boots in the Southwest, white suits in the Southeast, Mexican clothing around Amarillo. This type of clothing is "owned" by the locals, and if outsiders wear the local uniform they are looked upon as phonys or put-ons.

When selling in the South, if you are visiting a particular business office for the first time, the safest combination of clothing would be a medium-range solid-blue suit, a white shirt and any discreet, conservative tie other than the polka-dot or Ivy League. The second best combination is a medium-range solid-gray suit, a pale blue shirt and a maroon tie, either solid or in a conservative pattern. Since both combinations allow the use of the same shoes and socks, and since they are acceptable almost anywhere in the country (except the Midwest), they are perhaps the best basic wardrobe for any salesmen who must travel widely in their jobs. A third recommended suit for the South, for summer and winter, is the traditional solid beige. With the exceptions of bankers' conferences and Wall Street offices, the solid beige is probably the best single suit in any part of the country, although the weights and textures should be compatible with the climate.

In the South, there are entire industries in which short sleeve shirts are acceptable because of the heat. I would suggest, however, that salesmen dealing with men in these industries wear their long sleeves and perspire, unless they are very friendly with the men they are selling to.

Suit-lapel and tie widths, as well as shirt collar sizes, at present seem to have standardized throughout the country. But if styles begin to change again, all men should be aware that it took most of the South two and a half years to adopt the wide lapel after it was standard attire in New York City. Such time lapses between regions must be taken into account.

Southerners who travel in the North, particularly into the Northeast, and even some who have business in the West, should pay attention to several rules:

1. Several very bright colors and patterns in suits are acceptable in the South on a year-round basis but only as summer wear in the North. Even though these may be all-weather suits, I strongly suggest solid or pinstripe grays and blues when doing business in the North, the pinstripe being reserved for the most conservative areas.

2. Men from the Southwest who wear Mexican or Western attire in their home territory should not wear such clothes anywhere else, because these will be looked upon as attire for rubes and will hurt credibility when selling serious merchandise or services.

WHAT WORKS BEST IN THE MIDWEST

The Midwest tradition for conservative attire is exaggerated and somewhat misleading, particularly in sportswear. (For the purposes of this discussion this area includes all the territory which is traditionally considered the Midwest, plus the states of Washington and Oregon, where reactions to clothes are basically the same). The Midwestern businessman is much more lively than his East Coast equivalent, although his reaction to salesmen is very unusual, varying tremendously from the rest of the country. Although the Midwesterner dresses conservatively by almost any standards—wearing grays and blues himself—he reacts negatively to men wearing solid gray suits, and doesn't react positively to men wearing solid blue suits. The best suit to wear in the Midwest for selling is a very tiny, shadow plaid. Brown suits also test well in the Midwest, although they trigger strong negative results throughout the rest of the country.

Men in the Midwest have very strong color prejudices. Whether you live there or are coming from the outside, never wear gold when selling. Don't wear gray, particularly in shirts or ties. Wear no purple or lavender and make certain that you wear nothing that identifies you, correctly or incorrectly, as a member of the Eastern elitest establishment.

It is absolutely impossible to sell in the Midwest if you wear any clothing that indicates you are not doing well financially. The Midwesterner reacts positively to signs of affluence and money, and it is the only section of the country where even poor taste can be effective for salesmen as long as it's expensive poor taste. Any salesman can drive a flashy car and wear the loud but obviously expensive suit to his heart's content.

Although almost every salesman I've ever met who works the Midwest travels in polyester suits, the upper echelon executives in Chicago and in a few corporate headquarters through the rest of the Midwest are very much into a rich, deep gray flannel look. If you are dealing with these men, you should dress accordingly. My final point about the Midwest is that it is anti-big city—against anyone who is too sharp, too perfect, too beautiful, too sophisticated, too anything that they are not.

THE SPECIAL CALIFORNIA DRESS CODE

Like almost everything else in California, its dress code is distinctly its own. In San Francisco, the code is somewhat formal, but in the southern areas of the state, informality prevails and extends deep into the business world. When selling in this area, it is absolutely taboo to wear pinstripe suits or any dark suit, unless you've been to a particular business twice before and seen executives wearing such attire on both occasions. As I said at the outset of this book: Common sense is the first rule.

The suits that work best in California are medium-range solids. Shirts may be much more colorful, and patterns that are taboo elsewhere are perfectly acceptable. The designs and patterns of ties are also much more lively. President Ford's ties, which are much too gaudy for the rest of the country, are conservative business ties in a large part of California.

Much of California business, particularly industries that have never been noted for being conservative, has adopted dress codes best described as bizarre. I once knew a carpet salesman who was exceptionally successful in California and used a wardrobe consisting of a velvet jacket, slacks and a shirt open a fair way down. Impressed with his abilities, he decided to conquer the greener pastures of New York. By his third day on the job his boss had already received two calls objecting that the previous salesman had been replaced by a "homosexual."

The biggest mistake made by salesmen in California is not that they ignore California dress codes, but that they go along too far with them. In entire industries, no one wears suits; no one wears ties; turtlenecks are very in and the leisure suit is considered rather dressy. Salesmen coming from other parts of the country, and even some local salesmen who are selling important products or services, think they can dress the same. This is not true. If you are selling your services as an accountant to a California firm that maintains very liberal dress codes, you should still dress as accountants do pretty much everywhere, because people in certain professions are expected to dress in certain ways and will encounter negative reactions if they dress in ways that run counter to expectations.

THE NORTHEASTERN LOOK

The last—but hardly the least—section of the country that operates under a special set of dress rules is the Northeast (excluding major corporate headquarters). In the Northeast, three dicta are basic: Be conservative; be traditional; be neat. If you obey those three, you really should have no problems, although it is also important in this part of the country not to be any more up to date in your clothing than the people you are dealing with.

The Northeast is still the bastion of the dark conservative

business suit, and the best is a solid dark blue. The best shirts are solid white or solid blue, and the best ties are rep, polka-dot and club.

AGE MAKES PLENTY OF DIFFERENCE

When the age of a buyer is over forty-eight, it is essential that the seller dress in the following manner, assuming that he is over thirty-three:

He should have no long sideburns and no hair covering his ears. His best suit is a conservative solid or pinstripe blue, anywhere in the country. Solid white and solid blue are the only absolutely safe shirts, because many men over forty-eight react negatively even to subtle stripes in shirts.

Ties that are always acceptable to this group of men are solid, rep and club. In the Northeast, and in corporate headquarters, the Ivy League tie is also acceptable. Although men over forty-eight may themselves wear very gaudy ties reminiscent of patterns and colors acceptable in their youth, salesmen can do so only at considerable risk.

Men over forty-eight will make some judgments about your socioeconomic standing and your competence based on your clothing, though not as strongly as younger men make. But the older fellows do make very strong *moral* judgments based on clothing. So if part of your sales job is to be highly credible, the rules must be strictly obeyed. This also holds true for men selling products involving questionable credibility to begin with —such as used cars.

There are several exceptions to the rules. Some men over forty-eight, particularly those who have not reached the upper levels of the company, tend to be quite defensive against younger men who are within ten years of their own age. So salesmen from age thirty-eight up should generally not wear pinstripe suits and high authority ties, but stick with something softer.

Men who are under thirty-three and selling to men over forty-eight cannot be too authoritative because their extreme youth works against them. Therefore it is essential that the younger man wear only the highest authority garments—the pinstripe suit, vests, wingtip shoes—and that he conduct himself in a very businesslike manner.

In numbers as well as influence, the largest group of men in industry to whom someone must sell are the men between the ages of thirty-four and forty-seven. These men will not make strong moral or credibility judgments based on your clothing. But they do place much value on the socioeconomic level of your clothing. The most important general rule with this group is to wear only upper-middle-class clothing if you do not know the background of the man you are dealing with. If you do know that a man comes from a lower class, some items of neutral clothing (solid or rep ties, for example) are often effective, and the obviously upper-middle-class club tie and pinstripe suit should be avoided.

Men over forty-eight who are selling to buyers between ages thirty-four and forty-seven should frequently wear plaid suits, since their age carries its own authority. The younger men are accustomed to reacting to older men as authority figures and will resent the man who comes on too authoritatively when selling to them.

If a man between the ages of thirty-four and forty-seven is selling to men in the same age group, the general rules apply. If a younger man is selling to this group, he should attempt to dress at their age level rather than his. It is not necessary that he cut his hair as short as theirs, but it should be neat, and his ears should not be covered. He should always wear suit jacket, shirt and tie, and follow all the rules of manners that the older men adhere to.

If you are selling to men from twenty-eight to thirty-four, and you are in that age group, dress codes are basically unimportant, except that you should not dress as if you are much older. If you are older than these men, they will expect you to dress according to your own age category. Men between the ages of twenty-eight to thirty-four seem to have no significant prejudices against any patterns or colors.

How to Use Clothes to Sell Yourself

DRESS PREJUDICES OF COLLEGE STUDENTS

On the other hand, the prejudices of college students are violent and strong. If you turn off a college student with your clothing, you turn him off completely. There are no degrees; they either love you or hate you. College students expect you to fit the stereotype they have of you. If you sell rock and roll, you must look the part. College students have very strong prejudices against anyone in their own age group who does not obey the uniform of nonconformity of the day. College students react negatively to certain items, for which I have no explanations. One no-no is the solid blue suit; it's death on a campus, as are pinstripe suits, Ivy League and club ties.

If you are recruiting or you are selling something important (or something they identify as important) to college students, the best outfit is a solid gray suit, blue shirt and rep tie. They also react positively to paisley ties. The one rule you can never break when selling to college students is that if you are obviously out of their age category, you should not attempt to emulate their dress patterns or styles; they will distrust you if you do. If you are selling anything that is not profit-oriented, the slightly seedy, slightly rumpled professorial look works well. People who sell profit-oriented goods should look the part.

WHEN BLACKS SELL TO WHITES (AND VICE VERSA)

The following paragraphs have nothing to do with racial prejudice. I use race as a sociological term. I do this because racial terms are often the best indicators of common past environment and therefore one of the best predictors of present reaction to stimuli by an identifiable group. In the same way that parents and communities pass on their tastes for certain types of food, they also pass on concepts of honesty, fair play, etc. If these concepts are associated in their minds with certain types of clothing, they will also pass on this association. Therefore if you wish to sell to a group of people, it would be helpful to know which colors and patterns their environment has taught them to trust and which ones to distrust. That is all I have attempted to measure.

When selling to white middle America, and this includes anyone who is white and not in a ghetto or in a subgroup such as Appalachian mountainfolk, the following rules always apply: Never wear purple or lavender. Never wear loud colors. Never wear bright red, even in a tie. Pink shirts, except for end-on-end or Oxford cloth, are taboo. Don't wear jewelry. Don't have hair that covers your ears.

If you're a black selling to white middle America, dress like a white. Wear conservative pinstripe suits, preferably with vests, accompanied by all the establishment symbols, including the Ivy League tie. This clothing conveys that you are a member of the establishment and that you are pushing no radical or other feared ideas.

Blacks selling to whites should not wear Afro hair styles or any clothing that is African in association—that is, not if they want to sell.

If you are of Spanish origin (including Mexicans, Puerto Ricans, Cubans and Latin Americans), you should avoid pencil line mustaches, any articles of clothing that have Spanish associations, and anything that is very sharp or precise. Also avoid any hair tonic that tends to give a greasy or shiny look to the hair; this also triggers a strong negative reaction.

If you are white and selling to blacks, you will fare much better if you dress in nonestablishment patterns. Black America is essentially divided into two camps, establishment and antiestablishment, and the divisions are not dictated by income alone.

Almost all members of northern ghettos who are in lower socioeconomic groups are understandably disestablishment blacks. When selling to them, you can wear *nothing* that carries an establishment touch. It does not matter what you are selling —cars, insurance, bonds, gold—you must not wear the traditional suit, shirt and tie uniform. (Women are much better at selling to blacks because they are considered to be outside the establishment.)

White salesmen selling to antiestablishment blacks do better if they wear mustaches, and they do even better with beards. Leisure suits are better than business suits, but no suit should be solid dark blue. Turtleneck sweaters work very well, but if you must wear a tie, it should be an obviously nonauthoritative or nonestablishment one.

The black establishment includes all blacks who have made it, along with almost all southern rural blacks, no matter what their position. Southern blacks do not consider themselves disenfranchised, and their reactions to clothing are the same as the reactions of their more successful counterparts. If you are white and selling to this group, it is almost essential that you wear a shirt and tie, but it is absolutely essential that no article of your clothing represent you as a member of the establishment. Pinstripe suits, Ivy League and club ties, white shirts, are out. Conservative gray suits are fine; beige suits are better; any color shirt but white, and any nondescript tie are acceptable. A paisley tie is most likely to elicit the greatest trust.

When selling to middle-class blacks, you cannot dress like a ghetto black, and you cannot go so far into the antiestablishment look that you begin to affect beads or the like.

The one rule that applies to blacks just as it does to the white establishments in the Midwest and the South is that poverty does not sell. Blacks will believe people who look successful, which proves that everyone has one color-love in common, and that's green—not in clothes but inside your wallet.

Blacks selling to other blacks are best served by an entirely different set of dress codes. Conservative, establishment symbols of authority and success are the rules of the day. All blacks, regardless of their own status, react positively to other blacks who have made it.

Blacks selling to people of Spanish origin and people of Spanish origin selling to blacks should each avoid wearing any items of clothing that are particularly identified with the other group.

HOW TO SELL TO ETHNIC GROUPS

The following rules apply to anyone selling to ethnic groups.

When selling to upper-middle-class people of Spanish origin, it is essential that you dress both conservatively and nattily.

When selling to Jews, do not wear brown. When selling to older Jews, do not wear beige.

When selling to the basically German populations in the Midwest, avoid a clash in the lines of clothing patterns.

When selling to Polish groups in the Midwest, avoid a clash of color. Now I know there are many tasteless jokes about Poles wearing blue and red and green and yellow at the same time. I don't know any people of Polish origin who do this, but you certainly should never put this joke to a test.

Italians register negative reactions to clashes of color and clashes of line. The most conservative clothing sells best to Italians, and the richer-looking the better.

Although I tested for three years, I have been able to isolate absolutely no clothing prejudices among Orientals, although they dress very conservatively themselves.

Americans of Irish extraction react negatively to anyone who is too sharply dressed, too neat or put together too well. They associate such looks with being dishonest.

Mexican-Americans react negatively to anyone coming from outside the area, including other Mexicans, who wear what is best described as Mexican (bullfighters') red.

HOW TO FIT IN WITH YOUR CUSTOMER'S OCCUPATION

To sell successfully you must also wear clothes that are compatible with the occupation and education of your customers.

People who are trained in detail work and people who derive a sense of completion from their jobs, such as druggists, accountants and engineers, may buy from you whether you are dressed in Bermuda shorts or in a suit. But they give off very negative reactions to anyone whose dress does not add up to a harmonious unit.

They will not buy from you if you combine Bermuda shorts with wingtip shoes. If you are wearing a conservative shirt and conservative suit, but have a naked lady on your tie, they will object to you, not because of the naked lady, but because your clothing is not properly unified. The same tie with an equally ridiculous jacket would be just fine.

These men have a dominant sense of fitness and completion, and if you violate it, you become less credible and less important.

Artists, architects, hair dressers, scenic designers, window dressers—anyone who is trained as an artist or who considers himself an artist—will generally have a very strong sense of line. If the lines in your clothes clash, these people will think less of your credibility and judge you severely. They think better of someone who puts his clothes together cleverly than of someone who does not, but their concept of clever is far different from that of the average man.

What the average artist considers clever is a blue suit worn with a blue and green shirt and a blue and green tie—unusual, tricky combinations that do work. They are much more impressed with someone who might wear three shades of blue than someone who would wear a blue suit, white shirt and blue tie.

In selling to career military men, do not wear gray suits, do not wear Ivy League ties, do not wear business clothes at all if you can avoid it. You will do much better in sport jackets, golf jackets, etc., than in traditional business suits. Whatever you wear, military men react positively to outward signs of wealth and power.

Anyone who sells to government functionaries should know that there are two groups. Older bureaucrats who have worked themselves up from the depths of civil service react very negatively to any sign of wealth. The best way to dress for them can be described as shabby Brooks Brothers—clean, neat, but well worn. The younger breed of government officials still like a conservative look, but it does not have to be shabby. These men came into the government at fairly decent salaries, have moved up the socioeconomic ladder and dress much better themselves than their older counterparts to whom frugality is a way of life.

Generally when dealing with government officials, you should dress in Eastern establishment tradition, and avoid anything that marks you as being part of any special interest group, whether religious, political, social or fraternal.

Men who go into high appointed positions in government usually come from high socioeconomic backgrounds, and they take these jobs either because they need the money or because they already have all they need. These men react negatively to anyone from an obviously lower socioeconomic background, so one must dress for these elitists not only in upper-middle-class uniform, but in the obviously expensive version thereof.

Most corporate purchasing agents tend to fall into two general categories. Those who come from lower-middle-class homes represent about 60 percent of their profession in America. These are men with little formal education but considerable competence and they work their way up into authority over considerable budgets for a large variety of business needs. These men take to people who are conservative and reliable and distrust men who are too strong authority figures, so I recommend avoiding pinstripe suits, and sticking to the solid blue suit with rep tie.

The other group of purchasing agents make major corporate decisions. They buy computers, buildings, land sites, etc. They are very definitely executive-oriented men, and the standard executive dress code applies with them. The more authority you can generate, the better off you are.

Doctors, although they are quite conservative themselves, react well to salesmen wearing semi-casual attire and to up-to-date clothing. They react negatively to clothing that is out-of-date, and to people who are obviously poor.

Hospital administrators, on the other hand, generally come from lower socioeconomic backgrounds and react in much the same way as government bureaucrats. They like threadworn Brooks Brothers.

HOW SEX CAN HELP YOU SELL

Since this is a book for men, I will confine my comments on sex and clothing to male salesmen and female buyers. When selling to women, every other rule of dress goes right out the window. Gentlemen, note well the following.

Women react positively to any man who dresses in up-to-date fashions—and negatively to anyone who looks obviously dated. This does not mean that you can break the code of expectations. Say, you sell stocks and bonds. Then your women customers expect you to wear a pinstripe suit. The pinstripe should be gray with a white line, worn with a white shirt and a tie that picks up both colors. The combination is conservative, but it is also up-to-date and chic.

Most women hesitate to buy from (or even believe) any man who is very short.

Women react negatively to men who wear pink shirts or to any soft pastel color in any garment other than shirts. Women react positively to power colors on men, even though they would probably choose other colors for their own husbands. They will believe a man wearing a blue suit and a white shirt much more readily than they will give credence to a man in a light gray suit and a light blue shirt. Contrast gives a man much more credibility with women.

Women tend to believe men who are very large, so large men can sell more easily to women than average-sized men. They may also wear garments that make them look even larger or more powerful. Large men do not frighten women, and all signs of power are received in a positive way.

Women accord greater credibility to a man who puts his colors and lines together well and with great care. When a man does not do this well, women do not think that he doesn't care;

they think he doesn't know how, and they therefore minimize his ability in other areas.

Women generally dislike traditional items in clothing. Club ties and rep ties are best avoided; paisleys are good. White- and blue-solid shirts are best avoided, but pale yellow solids and patterns are acceptable.

All women should be treated as if they are of the uppermost socioeconomic bracket. They will respond better to Fifth Avenue clothes than to Seventh Avenue clothes, and even if you do not know the difference, you may count on this truism: Every women in America does know. This is astounding, but I tested this thesis with a group of third-grade ghetto girls and they knew the difference! I have a feeling that women are born with the knowledge.

When women buy items they feel require any kind of comparative economic decisions—items on which they normally try to save money—the salesman should not be dressed too expensively; if he is, women will immediately assume that he is making too much profit. With such items, lower-middle-class clothing for the salesman works much better with women in all categories except those who have absolutely no money worries.

Frequently salesmen tell me that they sell to too many different types of people to make my suggestions work. Generally this is not true. I suggest that any salesman who believes this make up a chart. On the chart, he should list every customer he meets in one month; the sales potential of each individual as well as the amount actually received from him; and the category of the buyer in terms of age, socioeconomic background and company orientation. This chart enables the salesman to get an overview of the people he's dealing with. It enables him to ration his time more carefully, giving more attention to those clients who could be even more important. And it also enables him to plan his days so that he sees one type of person on one day and a second type on the next.

I realize that some contradictions are built into my advice, say if you are selling to a Southerner who is over forty-eight. In such cases, you must use the clothing recommended to satisfy the most important factor. In descending order of importance, these factors are occupation, age and geography. From there on, your instincts are your best guide.

DRESSING TO MATCH YOUR PRODUCT

When Gerald Ford was minority leader of the House of Representatives, he sold his product—himself—excellently. He was Jerry the nice guy and he dressed like Jerry the nice guy. When he became President, he had a different product to sell— leader of the country—but he didn't change his image in the beginning of his presidency and was still projecting Jerry the nice guy. Unfortunately, great numbers of people were ignoring him with disdain. Obviously appearance is not the only reason but he had to change his image—and he did, successfully.

The point is: if you are a salesman—and even the President is one—you are not what you eat; *you are your product.* And you must dress accordingly.

I was once disseminating this advice to a group of salesmen when one jumped up and said, "I sell computers. How do you dress like a computer?" I then did a very quick analysis of the audience. I first asked if there were men present who did not sell computers. I then asked those men what they knew about computers. They answered that computers are expensive, efficient, yet they break down a lot.

I then told the salesman that he really wasn't selling a computer. What his client was buying when he chose between computers was the reliability and integrity of the company. If the salesman worked for IBM, the integrity was already set up through the company's reputation. If he worked for Joe Schmoe computers, the only way the buyer could judge the company was by the way he appeared, and therefore it would be helpful for him to dress in a way that would insinuate that his was a

143

very honest, reliable company that could back up its claims and give excellent service.

DO YOU KNOW WHAT YOUR TRUE PRODUCT IS?

The main problem with most salesmen dressing to suit their product is that they don't know what their true product is. They make the very poor assumption that the product is what it physically is. This is wrong. Salesmen must dress to suit *not what they are selling, but what people are buying.* The difference can be large and crucial.

I was once hired by a Cadillac dealer to help dress his sales force. He owned several dealerships throughout the country. One dealership dealt only with people who were quite rich. They were not buying Cadillacs; they were buying basic transportation. Like most upper-middle-class people, these customers trusted people who looked as if they were in the same income bracket, so we put the salesmen in good, conservative upper-middle-class attire, and their sales increased.

Several months later the owner called me back and said that he had dressed his salesmen in another dealership in the same way and was having trouble. When I visited the other dealership I found out why. That dealership was selling primarily to people who had considerably less money. They were not buying Cadillacs either; they were buying prestige. So we dressed up that group of salesmen with high-power-prestige apparel which conveyed that they had made it big. Sales improved.

Incidentally, I found in both dealerships that the most successful salesmen had been dressing correctly before I got there. Although we are talking about a fairly subtle difference in the appearance between the salesmen in the two agencies, that slight difference made a substantial difference in sales, because the buyers' frame of mind was substantially different. Here, then, is proof that the problem is not what is being sold; it's what is being bought.

With some products and sales methods, the point of customer attitude toward the person who sells the product is particularly significant. When working for insurance companies, I have found that salesmen who sell insurance to people from the lower-middle class had best not wear gray pinstripe suits, although they should look affluent. The very idea behind insurance (i.e., death) and the inevitable complexity and fine print of all policies scare lower-middle-class people, so if the salesman comes on as a very strong executive type, these people don't consider themselves able to hold a conversation with him. They are intimidated by his appearance and will turn him off long before he can close the sale. If he comes on as just a well-dressed neighbor, he fares much better.

HOW TO SELL DOOR-TO-DOOR

If a man is selling door-to-door, he must overcome the natural fear of women toward strangers before he even gets in the door. It would be a mistake for him to dress as an authority figure. He should look non-threatening by dressing in soft colors, with little contrast, and open his tie a bit at the collar. The door-to-door salesman of any item that costs real money should particularly keep in mind that he has one product to sell before he gets in the door, and one after he is inside. If he doesn't sell himself first, he'll never even get a chance to try selling what he really came to sell.

Salesmen selling to offices have a different problem. If they do not wear high authority garments, they either cannot get past secretaries and receptionists or are made to wait interminably because their importance is judged by their clothing. Expensive power garments can cut that waiting time by one-third to one-half, so there is that much more time left for selling.

Today, IBM and its symbol-laden white shirt remain first-glance indicators of success, prestige and reliability. But when IBM first started selling computers, the world of these expensive machines was a confusing, unreliable new field. The basic idea about computers in the minds of most people was that they were unreliable. The white shirt was a brilliant tactical move because it lent the look of reliability to the salesmen even if the product was trouble prone.

Used-car salesmen face the same problem. People are automatically suspicious of them (often with good reason), but I have found that by taking used-car salesmen out of their usually gaudy attire and putting them in blue blazers, gray pants, non-descript shirts and perhaps even a club tie with a small company logo or insignia, there is much less resistance to their sales pitch and people feel they are more credible. The look conveys a feeling of youth and innocence and it works.

When I am invited to speak before business organizations, I know that if the men present have only read about me in magazine articles or heard about me from someone else, they will automatically have me stereotyped as a fashion designer or consultant—someone who is frilly and flighty and unimportant. My standard wardrobe for such appearances is a pinstripe suit, usually with vest and very conservative tie. This clothing immediately suggests—accurately—that I am another business-man, just as they are; that I am a man of substance; and that I'm serious. This is how I am able to offset the negative connotations of my services before I even open my mouth.

Clothing can also be used further to enhance the existing positive associations of your business. If you work for a large, old corporation, and you dress very conservatively, your clothing will reconfirm the feeling in your clients that the company is still solid as a rock, reputable and doing quite nicely.

I once knew a man in Washington who sold packaged political campaigns. Since politicians are not known for giving much credence to the ideas of others, he knew he had to come on as a supreme authority figure. And he found that the best way to do it was to overwhelm them. He was a large man to begin with, but he reinforced his physique by wearing black suits with pin-stripes, a white shirt and black tie. And he overwhelmed people who weren't accustomed to being overwhelmed. He used a super hard sell, and his clothing added to his power and prestige.

DRESS RULES THAT ALWAYS PAY OFF

In addition to the general guidelines involving size, age, sex, race, socioeconomic background, geography, occupational orientation and product significance, there are some rules that all salesmen should adhere to, all the time. They are:

1. If you have a choice, dress affluently.

2. Always be clean; it is not always necessary to be obsessively neat, but it is always imperative to be clean.

3. If you are not sure of the circumstances of a selling situation, dress more—rather than less—conservatively than normal.

4. Never wear any item that identifies any personal association or belief, unless you are absolutely sure that the person to whom you are selling shares those beliefs. This rule includes school rings, masonic rings, ties that are connected with a particular area, political buttons, religious symbols, etc.

5. Always dress as well as the people to whom you are selling.

6. Never wear green.

7. Never put anything on your hair that makes it look shiny or greasy.

8. Never wear sunglasses, or glasses that change tint as the light changes. People must see your eyes if they're to believe you.

9. Never wear any jewelry that is not functional, and keep that simple. Big rings, bracelets and gaudy cuff links are absolutely taboo.

10. Never wear any item that might be considered feminine.

11. Wear, do or say something that makes your name or what you are selling memorable. Clothing or accessories are a very effective ploy in the identity game. I've had clients who wore fancy watches, or have always worn the same shade of shirt, and even men who wore two different cuff links (pointing them out to people as luck charms) to make sure that people do not forget them or their product easily.

12. If it is a part of your regalia, always carry a good attaché case.

13. Always carry a good pen and pencil, not the cheap, junky ones.

14. If you have a choice, wear an expensive tie.

15. Never take off your suit jacket unless you have to. It weakens your authority.

16. Whenever possible, look in the mirror before you visit a client. Although it sounds silly to be telling this to grown men, you'll be surprised at how many flaws you'll catch this way— hair out of place, tie slipped or badly tied, a stain on your shirt.

Make up a checklist of these admonitions, as well as any others that are important to your individual circumstances, and carry it with you at all times.

HOW TO TEST YOUR DRESS HABITS YOURSELF

If you are really serious about improving your sales, or judging your ability, you will also do the following:

For a period of thirty days, keep a running record of exactly what you wear every day. Keep your own record of the clothing worn by two other men in your company: one who does no better than you or does worse, and one of the more successful men in the company. At the end of thirty days, make a comparison. Is your clothing closer in appearance to the successful man or the unsuccessful man?

This simple test should change the dressing habits of half the salesmen in America who are not doing well.

When I speak before most sales groups, I can look out in a crowd and tell you who is selling and who isn't, merely by judging their dress. Sometimes I can even tell about a man by the way his wife is dressed.

The next test is a bit more complicated, but could be very enlightening. Have a friend take several pictures of you wearing what you usually wear, plus several of you in other clothes. Have the friend show it to people who do not know you. Ask them to judge your honesty, reliability, likability, etc. You may find that a change of wardrobe is definitely in order.

Never buy any article of clothing unless you believe that article will help you sell. I mean it should actively help, not just be neutral or of questionable value.

Test every suit you presently have by keeping a record of when you wear each one and how well you fare on those days.

How many doors were opened to you in your blue suit?

How long did you have to wait in the outer office in your gray suit?

What were people's reactions to you in your brown suit?

How much did you sell in your beige suit?

After six months of this, you may take a few of suits out and give them to charity.

Finally, I recommend that every morning before you leave home, you station yourself in front of a full-length mirror for a minute or preferably two. You don't have to do anything else. Questions about your dress will arise in your mind and, after some thought, will answer themselves. When you do this, give yourself about ten extra minutes to get out of the house, because you'll find yourself changing clothes on many mornings.

HERE'S MY PERSONAL GUARANTEE TO YOU

During hard times and tough sales, every salesman and every sales manager is particularly entitled to be cynical about all the advice I have given. Let me therefore put the following formal challenge into cold print.

I will take on half the salesmen of any sizable corporation; let the corporation take on the other half. Starting with the most successful salesman, the company gets the best man; I get the second best; the company gets the third best; I get the fourth; and this is carried out all down the line.

I guarantee that after the first year I can improve the sales of my group at least until its record exceeds by 5 percent the group that was previously leading. If I do not, then my services are free. All I ask is that my out-of-pocket expenses be covered, I receive a reasonable percentage of any new profits I create, and I am able to meet with at least twenty members of the sales force each day.

I can do this with no fear of loss because I know that merely by changing the physical appearance of salesmen, I can substantially increase their sales in the majority of cases.

8.

SOME ADVICE FOR MINORITIES

It is an undeniable fact that the typical upper-middle-class American looks white, Anglo Saxon and Protestant. He is of medium build, fair complexion, with almost no pronounced physical characteristics. He is the model of success; that is, if you run a test, most people of all socioeconomic, racial and ethnic backgrounds will identify him as such. Like it or not, his appearance will normally elicit a positive response from someone viewing him. Anyone not possessing his characteristics will elicit a negative response in some degree, regardless of whether that response is conscious or subconscious.

I once had a man come to me who said, "I'm a reasonably successful, honest businessman, but everyone thinks I'm a gangster."

He did have a very harsh, gruff appearance, and since gangsters, and our stereotypes of them, tend to come from a lower-middle-class background and look accordingly, I had the man dress consistently in upper-middle-class garments—pinstripe suits with vests, conservative shirts, Ivy League ties. Because his harsh features seemed to scare or intimidate people, I also tried to give him as soft a look as possible, avoiding dark colors and strong contrasts, and using instead such combinations as a pale gray pinstripe suit with a very pale blue shirt and muted tie. The look was extremely successful for him, and thereafter his appearance did not detract from his position.

His problem was very similar to that of many executives who come from a Mediterranean background: They look rather harsh by American standards. The best advice I can give to men with such problems is that they stay with very soft colors and textures, wear very traditional styles, and affect the appurtenances of success.

The two groups who have the most problems with their appearance are blacks and men of Spanish background. It is unfortunate but true that our society has conditioned us to look upon members of both groups as belonging to the lower classes, and no matter how high a minority individual rises in status or achievement he is going to have some difficulty being identified by his success rather than by his background.

But clothing can help. For years I have been giving the following advice to my black and Spanish clients: Dress conservatively; wear only those garments that are considered upper-middle-class symbols—pinstripe suits, end-on-end blue shirts, Ivy League ties; wear and carry only those accessories that convey the same message.

In speaking before some groups of black executives, I have been criticized for attempting to make "Uncle Toms" out of them. My only answer is that my black clients include officers of several of America's major corporations and representatives of foreign governments. They are hardly Uncle Toms. I stick to my advice. If you are black or Spanish in America, and if you are moving up the rungs of corporate success, you should adhere to the dress code of the corporation and of the country, even going somewhat overboard in the direction of being conservative.

This requirement of dress is not one that is imposed on you strictly because you are of a minority race; it is imposed on anyone who wishes to go up the corporate ladder. If you have to work harder at it than the white man next to you—well, so does the very short man with a larger man at the desk next to him. Consciously manipulating your dress for success is not giving in; it is a recognition by the man who is doing it that he deserves a crack at the upper echelons of business and he's going to play the same game everyone else is playing, even if he has to play a little harder.

Homosexuals also have a problem if they flaunt the clothing affectations often associated with their preferences. What a man does in his bedroom is private, but what he does in another man's corporation affects his bank balance and the other man's reactions. If you wish to proselytize for homosexual rights, go right ahead; you'll be doing a very good thing for generations to come. But if you want to succeed in the mainstream of American business, keep your sex life and your affectations in the closet.

9.

HOW TO GET THE MOST OUT OF ACCESSORIES

There are very successful men in this country who wear expensive suits, expensive shirts, expensive ties, and who drive expensive cars. Some of these men are $100,000 a year pimps and some are $100,000 a year corporate executives. Without seeing them and merely having their major articles of clothing identified as expensive, we would find it difficult to distinguish between them. By describing their accessories, we would know the difference immediately.

The word "accessories" implies items that are nonessential. But it is very often *because* they are nonessential that accessories are so important to the overall look of the successful man. I am sure that my advice will be of little interest to pimps, but it is crucial to legitimate businessmen.

WHAT TO DO ABOUT JEWELRY

The basic rule about men's jewelry is the less the better. Too much jewelry, or the wrong jewelry, will be considered effeminate or foppish and elicit strong negative responses from most people.

154

Collar pins, while they check out in my research as evoking neither positive nor negative reactions, are seriously out-of-date and do not work well with wide ties.

Tie clips are unnecessary, passé and nowadays in poor taste. They should never be worn. The same is true of stickpins. One out of a thousand men might find a stickpin useful to call attention to himself if he has a severe presence problem, but if he does wear one, it'd better be tasteful and extremely expensive.

Lapel pins should be worn only if they are significant. If you do not know what lapel pins are significant, then don't wear them.

Some men can get away with wearing very discreet, expensive and tasteful I.D. bracelets. Very few men (or bracelets) fall into this category. Stay away from them.

The only completely acceptable ring is the wedding band. Period.

Cuff links should be simple and small. The most acceptable cuff link is the solid gold or solid silver ball or any variation of it. Cuff links should never be large or gaudy; if you must wear stones, at least wear real ones.

Within reason, there are no unacceptable belts; the buckle is the problem. Big, heavy or ornate buckles tend to be unacceptable; small, clean, traditional buckles with squared lines are best (see drawing below).

Belts
for Business

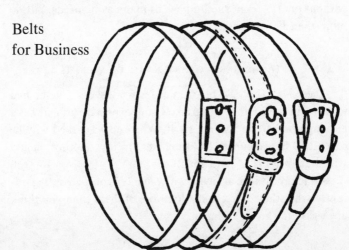

The only other acceptable pieces of jewelry of any kind are money clips; if they are simple, elegant and tasteful, money clips evoke positive responses.

The only item a man should wear around his neck is a tie —no beads, chains or medallions, regardless of their connotation or meaning, not even with sport clothes and not even in bathing suits. If you want to wear anything other than a tie around your neck, go into show business.

GETTING THE MOST OUT OF WALLETS

All wallets are okay, but the larger, longer "pocket secretary" that can only be carried in the suit pocket is definitely an upper-middle-class symbol; others are only neutral (see drawing on page 157). Regardless of what kind of wallet you carry, it should never be so crammed full of junk that it bulges.

In wallets, as in all other leather goods, the finer the leather, the better it will work for your overall presence. The best color for wallets is a dark, rich brown—almost cordovan color, but not quite.

Speaking of wallets, credit cards, particularly prestigious ones like American Express, are signs of success and are regarded as such by all classes. They are essential to any businessman (you have probably noticed that you can hardly rent a car without one). A man should have as many as he needs, but no more than he can afford.

ATTACHE CASES CARRY A LOT OF WEIGHT

There is a story of a black minister who, every time he had to travel in the South, carried an elegant, expensive attaché case, although he had no real use for it. When he was asked why he carried it, he explained: "Without it, I'm just another nigger; with it, I'm a black gentleman."

Attaché cases are always positive symbols of success, regardless of what they carry, and a lot more of them than you think are used only to carry lunch.

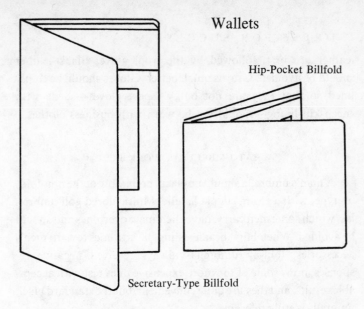

Wallets

Hip-Pocket Billfold

Secretary-Type Billfold

All attaché or brief cases are acceptable, but the most acceptable are the ones made in a dark, rich, almost-cordovan tone of brown leather. Any other shade of brown comes next. Black and gray test the worst. Attaché cases should be plain, simple and functional, with no decoration or obtrusive hardware.

MAKING THE MOST OUT OF PENS

All businessmen should carry a pen, pencil or both. There is very definitely an executive, important look to some pens, and the look is thin silver or gold. Under no circumstances should a man use a cheap pen or pencil in the presence of other men, although a lot do. You may think that this is an insignificant point; comparatively speaking, it is, but no man who writes with a $25 pencil will ever be considered poor or a slob. If he writes with a $.25 one he might be.

HOW TO HANDLE GLOVES

Every gentleman has several sets of gloves; every man should have. Almost all gloves are appropriate, but rich, brown leather are best, followed by the wool glove. Black leather should be avoided. Gray is much better. Gloves should be thinly lined so that they are not bulky. Sport gloves—suede with sheepskin lining—should not be worn with business clothes.

WHAT UMBRELLAS WORK BEST

A man's umbrella should be black, preferably of the non-fold-up type, with a clean, simple handle. Multicolored golf umbrellas, which some men carry, have effeminate overtones and should be avoided. When I first began testing the attitudes toward men's accessories, fold-up umbrellas always received negative responses; now, some of the more expensive ones test with acceptable results, and they are quite convenient, but the standard black umbrella is still preferable.

WHAT SCARVES ARE ACCEPTABLE

Acceptable scarves are made of silk and wool, no other materials. Some silk scarves are reversible, with wool on the facing side. The predominant patterns of silk scarves are foulard and solids; plaids and solids dominate in the wool versions. Almost any pattern or color is acceptable in scarves as long as it is not gaudy. If you are not sure, leave it alone, unless it would also be an acceptable tie pattern. White scarves are generally too dressy for day use.

HANDKERCHIEF DO'S AND DON'TS

Men's handkerchiefs should be cotton or linen, hand rolled and white. Handkerchiefs worn in the breast pocket of the suit are not uncommon among older men and are perfectly acceptable with conservative suits. Very young men who wear pocket handkerchiefs tend to look affected. Colored handkerchiefs, or handkerchiefs that match ties should be worn by no one.

158

SHOES THAT WORK

Acceptable colors for business shoes are black, brown and cordovan. Patent leather is acceptable only for men in glamour industries, and I would question their use even there. The wingtip and other plain lace shoes are the traditional footwear of the American businessman, although slip-ons are acceptable if they are not gaudy, and if they do not have too much metal on them.

The Most Popular Looks in Executive Footwear

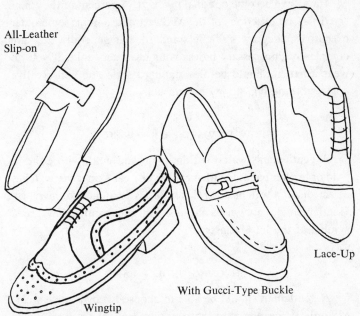

All-Leather
Slip-on

Lace-Up

With Gucci-Type Buckle

Wingtip

In the most ultrasophisticated cities, shoes with tassels, or shoes with Mr. Gucci's rather chic initial are perhaps—just possibly—acceptable for some men. Elsewhere they should be studiously avoided.

Multicolored shoes or those with high heels or platform soles should never be worn for business. A very short man may wear high-heels or lifts, but only with the most conservative shoes, never on anything that would call attention to the fact that he's wearing them.

THE RULE ABOUT SOCKS

Business socks should be dark and over-the-calf, never only ankle length or even slightly droopy. Ever.

THE ANTI-HAT REVOLUTION

Hats have become optional in about 95 percent of the country. In certain sections of the Midwest and among some older executives, they are still the standard, but generally they are completely unnecessary unless your head gets cold. If you do wear a hat, it should be of a standard style and conservative color, nothing big, floppy or unusual.

HOW TO WATCH YOUR WATCH

A gentleman's watch is thin, plain and gold, with either a gold or leather band. Gentlemen do not wear skin-diver watches or astronaut's watches or Mickey Mouse watches to the office. Gentlemen do not wear cheap expansion bands; they are a symbol of the lower classes.

CHOOSING UNDERWEAR

A gentleman should be able to choose his own underwear. My only suggestion is to the men who wear the same T-shirts for sport wear and business. Buy V-neck shirts; it won't matter under a shirt and tie, but your T-shirt should never show under an open-collared shirt.

PICKING OUTERWEAR

Four types of coats are acceptable: the car coat or suburban coat (which is basically for sports wear), the overcoat, the raincoat and the topcoat. Solid colors in outerwear are the most acceptable, and they go farther in any wardrobe.

For business wear, two overcoats are always acceptable, the camel hair and the slightly more dressy blue cashmere. Both are soft and rich, and go with almost anything.

Overcoats are not cheap, and if you have one at all, it should be a good one. The reason for making such an investment is tailoring. An overcoat should fit as well as a suit. Unless you are a perfect size, cheaper overcoats will not fit as they should, and cheaper stores will make only the most minimal adjustments. Better stores will tailor them to your specifications, and those specifications should be just as exacting as for your suits.

Topcoats are not as popular as they once were, but are worn in states where the weather never gets really cold, but some kind of coat is occasionally needed. Beige and blue are the most appropriate colors.

The beige raincoat, as you learned in Chapter 1, is *the* raincoat of the upper-middle class. As I've said, blue is okay, but black is never acceptable.

If you are a perfect build, you may buy any cut of coat you wish. If you are very short or very tall, you should never buy outerwear that stops just above the knees. On the short man, such a cut makes him look dumpy. On the tall man, it makes him look so tall that he seems to be stretching out of his coat.

Avoid fur collars on coats unless you can afford the very best and unless your only business is conducted in the most sophisticated cities.

Suede is acceptable in outerwear, although it is expensive and not very serviceable. Leather is acceptable, in shades of brown. Black leather is not acceptable, and has very negative connotations in our society.

10

THE DO'S AND DON'TS OF
SPORT CLOTHES AND FORMAL
WEAR

A few years ago, a major Midwestern corporation hired me to consult with them on uniforms for those of their employees who dealt with the public. While I was working at company headquarters, the president of the firm asked to see me, not because he was interested in what uniforms I was choosing, but because he wanted to discuss my clothing research for executives. After I had run through my standard fifteen-minute orientation, he said that he found my ideas quite interesting because he had always used clothing as a key to help him determine what executives he would move into the home office with him.

It was his practice to bring all young up-and-comers to the home office for several months. During that period he furnished them housing and a temporary membership in his country club. They all knew they were there to be watched, but they never knew how. He said that it really wasn't a question of ability; these men all had plenty of it because he had many more employees with ability than he had key positions. So the way he made his choice was principally by how they dressed in their leisure hours at the country club, his contention being that if they fit in there, then they would have no trouble fitting in at the office.

A second anecdote relevant to this discussion involves a Russian princess of my acquaintance. When I knew her, she was selling mutual funds, and very successfully. She always sold at a country club. When I asked her how she knew who her best potential buyers were, she said, "Simply by watching them play golf."

"Does the score count?" I asked.

"No," she replied, "but the clothing does."

And she was right. Within ten minutes on a golf course, she could not only estimate with fair accuracy who had money, but also whether it was old money or new money. Clothes were the key.

HOW SPORTSWEAR HELPS BUSINESS SUCCESS

To every man of substance, and to every man trying to achieve it, sportswear is often just as meaningful as business wear. Everybody knows that a tremendous amount of business —and often the most important business of all—is conducted during leisure activities in this country, and the judgments that are made about the qualities of men during their leisure time can be just as severe and just as crucial as those made during business hours.

The first rule of sportswear is that you should have some. The difference between men who are established in the upper-middle class and those who are not is probably most noticeable in their sportswear, because men who wear suits and ties to the office every day find it impractical and boring to wear the same type of apparel when engaging in physical activity or leisure pursuits. Therefore they tend to buy apparel specifically for leisure wear.

To make the most of your sportswear, all of it should be immediately distinguishable as such. Almost any single garment that may be of business use is incorrect, and so is almost any combination that is not totally composed of distinctly nonbusiness garments. To belabor the obvious: Wingtip shoes do not go with jeans; desert boots and sneakers do. Dress shirts do not go with walking shorts.

One of the distinguishing features of sportswear is color, which is definitely bright and sometimes even gaudy, although this does not mean that the general rules of good taste can be discarded. It is the mistaken belief of many men that once they put on sportswear they may combine garments in any helter-skelter way they choose. Not so. The basic business rule of not putting patterns against patterns is equally sound for sportswear, and colors that clash are colors that clash, regardless of their use. Poorly matching patterns and colors in sportswear, or even mixed styles of sportswear can be as detrimental to a man as the same faux pas in business wear.

COLORS TO AVOID

There are certain colors in sportswear that tend to lead to difficulties. Surprisingly, one of the colors that usually looks cheap, and therefore inappropriate, is light blue. Anything that falls into the category of light or sky blue tends to have negative connotations, while anything that falls into the category of baby blue tends to evoke good vibrations. If you're not sure which is which, avoid light blue.

Harsh or bright yellow should also be avoided; if you wish to wear yellows in sportswear, they should be pale and soft.

Maroon is better than red; the darker the red, the better it tends to work. Purple is a poor idea, regardless of the shade. Orange is almost impossible to match, except with another orange or white. Green and gold are not always bad, but they are negative 90 percent of the time, for a variety of reasons, and therefore make bad color choices.

The best colors in sportswear—the ones that are always safe —are navy blue, white, maroon, khaki and beige. If you use them, you'd have to try very hard to go wrong. The brighter colors are acceptable, sometimes even preferable (in ski wear, for example), as long as you understand that they must be properly coordinated and in good taste.

Materials and textures have a very definite effect on sportswear. You should always avoid silk, velvet and velour (although velour shirts are acceptable in winter). Any material that is so sheer that it can be seen through registers strongly negative. The best looks in material and texture are denim and the look of real cotton and real wool. Sportswear made of synthetics must be of the best quality, because anything less looks cheap and awful. As a general rule, synthetic sport garments should have the look of cotton or wool, with the exception of ski clothing, which because of its nature and purpose must be and look synthetic.

SPORTSWEAR PATTERNS: GOOD AND BAD

The best patterns in sportswear are solids and plaids. Circles, dots and stripes are generally bad. Any pattern that is busy, wild or moves in multiple directions is bad. Any pattern that looks as if it should be on a rug rather than on a garment is bad.

Good leather works very well for sportswear. Cheap leather is good for nothing. Other than belts, shoes and, occasionally, gloves, no leather garment should be black. Leather jackets that cut in and stop at the waist—the Eisenhower style, for example —tend to trigger a strong negative response.

The two basic mistakes that most men make with leisure wear concern quality and fit. Cheap sportswear is lower-middle-class-sportswear and looks it. It is inappropriate when it is new; it bags and sags and fades and doesn't last, and in the end is more expensive than if you had bought good quality to begin with. Every man should spend comparatively as much for his sportswear as he does for his business wear.

WHY FIT IS EXTRA IMPORTANT

Sport clothing should fit as well as, if not in some cases better than, business clothing. If a garment does not fit, have it carefully fitted by a tailor. The reason why sport clothing should often fit better is the bright colors and patterns and sharp contrasts that are hallmarks of most sport clothing. If the jacket of a conservatively colored and patterned suit is slightly too long, this is often unnoticeable because the jacket and pants tend to blend into each other. But with a boldly patterned sport jacket, worn with sharply contrasting slacks, the slightest flaw is immediately noticeable. Shirts and slacks, especially, must often fit better because no jacket goes over them to hide any problems. One of the most obvious fit problems with sport clothes involves very tall or very short men wearing walking shorts. With the short men, the shorts are very often too long and must be tailored up. The tall man will usually have to buy his walking shorts in special tall man shops so that they are long enough.

If a man knows absolutely nothing about sport clothing, and does not wish to learn, then the most important advice I can give him is to always buy the best garments in the best, most established and traditional stores. Granted, that is expensive advice, but it works. Line up ten men in various sport outfits from Sears and Roebuck, Brooks Brothers and Abercrombie and Fitch, and I will tell you which is which. It is not that the clothing from Sears will always be wrong, but that the clothing from Brooks and Abercrombie will almost never be, provided that the correct type of clothing is chosen for the appropriate occasion.

Since all acceptable sport clothing must have the upper-middle-class touch, the most acceptable looks are those that are traditional to the leisure pursuits of that class. Since leisure pursuits and looks are basically seasonal, I will describe the acceptable looks in seasonal order, beginning with winter.

GO FOR THE BRITISH LOOK

On any winter day, if you stand on Fifth Avenue in New York, you can spot any number of men wearing clothing that is much more at home on grouse hunts in the British Isles than on Fifth Avenue. There have not been many grouse on Fifth Avenue recently, and most of the men in those clothes wouldn't know which end of the gun to fire if there were targets available. But this is beside the point. The point is that we are basically Anglophiles in our clothing, particularly in sportswear, and so the look is absolutely acceptable.

The look has many variations, but it is basically beefy or tweedy, heavy and British. Jackets are of heavy tweeds or wide-wale corduroy, frequently with leather or suede patches, or they are reversed sheepskin. Slacks are of heavy wool, in either tweeds or subdued plaids. Shirts are heavy wool in Scottish plaids, and look like lumberjack shirts, except no lumberjack could afford one. Socks are heavy wool, and scarves are very tweedy or feature tartan plaids. Gloves are sheepskin lined. Shoes are generally neutral suede, and are very often high-topped. Fisherman's knit or Irish knit sweaters in off-white or light beige are part of the look, as are other very heavy sweaters in either navy or maroon.

Combined with this look are leather coats; rich, expensive cotton velour shirts (never, ever buy cheap velour); heavy worsted or herringbone suits; good turtleneck sweaters; and Russian fur or Swiss mountain climbing hats—now you have the basic staples of a gentleman's winter sport wardrobe.

THE SKI LOOK

The other specific winter look that is acceptable is the ski look. Almost all ski garments are bright nylon, and while some of the garments tend to look a bit out of place for street wear, skiing is a very "in" sport and the garments are quite acceptable as sports attire. Although no negative connotations are set off by older men wearing ski clothing, the look is basically young, and one rarely sees it on men over fifty.

The one acceptable sports look that bridges all seasons even though it is not really allied with any specific leisure activity is denim. Almost every type of garment imaginable is made from it, and almost all of them are acceptable.

THE EQUESTRIAN LOOK

The next acceptable sports look is the one associated with horseback riding. If there is an aristocratic tradition in America, horsemanship is part of it. Because of their easier accessibility to the masses, most other traditional upper-class sports have now been appropriated by the lower classes, but horseback riding largely remains the province of the rich or landed gentry, particularly in large cities and suburbs. Equestrian garments therefore tend to be upper-class symbols and are perfectly acceptable sportswear—on the way to the stable and back. If you don't know what appropriate riding garments look like, then you have no business buying them.

THE SPORTS CAR LOOK

A hybrid between riding clothes and the British country gentleman look is the combination affected by sports-car enthusiasts. Composed generally of a well-fitting tweed jacket, cavalry twill pants, a hand-knit, rustic-looking sweater, jodhpur boots, a tweed cap and open-backed racing gloves, this "look" really exists more in fiction than in fact, although it is seen occasionally in the Hamptons on the owners of $35,000 sports cars. Like equestrian gear, it really says that the wearer has a higher-class mode of transportation than the rest of us. Owners of Volkswagens and other fundamental means of transportation should avoid it.

Although no longer the exclusive property of the upper-middle class, golf, tennis and boating (from sailing to yachting) are still associated with some degree of success, and the right attire naturally has to be acceptable for spring, summer and fall.

THE TENNIS LOOK

The easiest is the classic tennis look composed of white short shorts, a white knit shirt with collar, a white sweater if necessary, white socks and white tennis sneakers. The only acceptable touches of color are maroon and navy stripes, usually only one of each, on each garment. Off the court, the shorts are exchanged for white duck pants. In some of the snootier country clubs, anything other than strict adherence to the above combination is verboten and considered a sign of the wearer's bad taste and less than acceptable background. In more informal settings, generally those not dominated by the old rich, almost any pair of solid color shorts and any knit shirt with collar are acceptable.

GOLF? OF COURSE!

Since golf is still pretty much the one game played by most upper-middle-class men and most industry executives, the right look for it is most important for any man trying to achieve success. As a matter of fact, this is the one game I would advise every young man on his way up make an effort to learn. It can easily take years to impress your superiors in the formal setting of the office, but much less time in the camaraderie of the golf course. I dare say that almost as many important corporate decisions in this country are made on the golf course as in the office, and if you can't be there because you can't play, then you can't be a part of the decision-making process.

Needless to say, the proper golf look is definitely upper-middle class, although there are tremendous variations from location and location, from old money to new money, and from clique to clique. The only way to learn what is acceptable to the group you're interested in joining is to observe carefully and assimilate quickly.

The mistake made by most golf enthusiasts is that they tend to overdo in amassing the equipment, gadgets and doodads associated with the game. The only essential pieces of equipment are clubs, balls and shoes. Everything beyond that tends to be nonfunctional. Such semifunctional items as the golf hat and golf gloves are not essential but acceptable. And the clothing worn on the golf course tends to be a man's everyday leisure clothing.

Old-money golfers seem to be just as happy in their well-worn Brooks Brothers chinos or corduroys and knit shirts as in anything else. With their golf shoes off, they look just as they might look while puttering around the garden or paying a Saturday visit to their favorite dispenser of spirits. New-money golfers tend to go more for the better, newer golf pants and golf shirts that are immediately identifiable as such because of their brighter colors, inevitable golf logos, or endorsement from everyone's favorite pro. The look carries over into the lightweight throwover golf jacket with crossed club insignia, and hats with the same. In addition, you can buy everything from club ties with crossed club insignias to pen and pencil sets with golf balls on the tops. As long as such items are expensive and in good taste, they are proper and acceptable, although they should never be overdone.

THE YACHTING LOOK

Yachting sportswear—the white pants and navy jacket with brass buttons and ascot or scarf—is dying, along with the old rich who so dearly loved it. Occasionally it is still seen around Palm Beach, sometimes in the Caribbean and about twenty times a day along the plushest ports of the Mediterranean. But unless you travel in those circles, on your own yacht and not someone else's, or you're practicing to become a seafaring gigolo, this is a look that is best left to your betters and to the geriatric set.

For the rest of us less-privileged salts, the best boating or sailing look is made up of sneakers, cotton pants and shirts of good cotton in light, pastel colors and denims.

There is very little to say about beach wear, since it is worn by every class in just about every style. About the only item that distinguishes the upper-class beach lounger from his less fortunate brothers is that, because of the requirements of the resorts he usually frequents, he wears a robe. The best advice on beach-wear is to buy in the most traditional stores and you will hardly ever be wrong.

Some clothing is basically sportswear with no specific use or look, except whatever is dictated by the season. This includes suits that are a bit too bright or too wildly patterned or of unacceptable material (corduroy in most occupations) to be worn for business wear. In the colder months or in the colder areas of the country, this clothing is not too difficult to choose: the right looks are basically woodsy, outdoorsy in compara-tively mild patterns and colors.

Solid navy or camel hair blazers are as conservative and as elegant as one can get in sport clothing, but they are still sport garments, and should seldom, if ever, be worn to the office with contrasting slacks. They are acceptable if worn with matching slacks, and these blazer suits are becoming more and more popular, particularly on Fridays when many men leave for the weekend directly from work. Because of its tremendous adapt-ability, a blazer suit with two extra pairs of pants and several different shirts or sweaters allow a man a decent, acceptable wardrobe for an entire weekend with a minimum number of garments.

In the South, and in the summer in other areas, a much more varied range of warm weather attire is acceptable. The most formal components are the many suits that can be worn to the office and then double as sportswear depending on the shirts, shoes, ties and accessories. I have illustrated this in Chapter 5, by showing a traditional summer pinstripe suit with a vest and a conservative tie, which is perfectly acceptable for business in any but the most formal offices. Changing the shirt to a plaid and tie to a bowtie, it becomes a very sporty outfit. It can be turned even sportier with dark brown pants, or, if you use the suit pants, white shoes and a white belt.

Most seersucker and cord summer suits give you this adaptability, and some denims also do, although denim is pretty much restricted to the glamour industries as a general rule.

The second variation of the summer look is the sport jacket with contrasting pants. Here we run into a great deal of difficulty, and here is where most men go wrong. Some men choose a sport jacket that is too conservative and looks as if it might be part of a suit. This should be strenuously avoided. Let me say it again: Sport clothing should look like sport clothing, and for the summer this means it should be quite lively with a bit of color in it.

Other men go too far in the other direction, and choose clothing that is too gaudy. In fact, many patterns and colors in summer sportswear are acceptable, but the best are solids and plaids. The plaids may be quite wild and even gaudy, as long as they are worn with calm, solid pants and as long as they are traditional in shape, detail and color.

The same rule that applies to putting business clothing together applies to combining items of sport clothing, only more so. Put solids next to patterns, and only wear one wild pattern in any outfit. Don't buy any patterns in any garment that are almost solid—no invisible plaid jackets and no raised weave ties.

In any season, with any sportswear, make sure that what you are wearing is a harmonious, acceptable unit. This means no dress shirts with walking shorts, no ski pants with British hacking jackets, no ties with knit shirts, no black, executive-length hose with white sailing pants.

THE USES OF LEISURE SUITS

According to the fashion industry, the leisure suit was a magnificent new idea created by that industry about three years ago. In fact, the leisure suit originated almost a century ago as the British army officer's uniform worn during the desert campaigns. When fashionable English gentlemen returned home from the wars, their battle jackets were very definite marks of status, and were frequently worn during leisure hours at their clubs.

Because of its comfort, ruggedness and easy adaptability, the jacket with its spacious pockets, mandatory belted waist and matching pants was soon adopted as standard attire by wealthy big-game hunters for their elaborate expeditions to Africa and India. The classic American version—always khaki colored, as were its predecessors—has been sold by Abercrombie and Fitch for years, and was popularized by Ernest Hemingway and other *macho* hunter/writers who found its rugged image and casual utility perfectly suited to their own needs.

If the fashion industry now wishes to call it a leisure suit, that's okay, but it was, in its beginnings in this country, a safari suit. It allowed American gentlemen to not hunt tigers and elephants in the same well-dressed manner that they affect when they do not hunt grouse. It was the spring version of the beefy British look, and was worn on Fifth Avenue by men who had never seen an elephant gun in their lives, but who were nonetheless members of the American aristocracy.

Thanks to the fashion industry's "new" idea and massive advertising campaigns in support thereof, the leisure suit now proliferates in a rainbow of colors (many of which heretofore were the exclusive province of the female of the species) and an abundance of styles and fabrics (including velvet; I have not yet seen any lace ones). This is what happens when aristocratic designs are made available to the masses. The general public insists that its basically lower-middle-class clothing prejudice be catered to, and each fashion designer pushes further and further out to stay ahead of his competitor. Although Mr. Hemingway and Mr. Abercrombie and Mr. Fitch must be turning over in their graves, the adaptations of their beloved suit have produced bizarre changes.

Regardless of my rather cynical attitude on this subject, the leisure suit still evokes the same class associations it always did and is perfectly acceptable attire for the American gentleman— *if* it is worn only for *leisure* and never for business (unless you are in a high-fashion business); *if* it is of a traditional khaki or more contemporary denim material; and *if* it follows the classic style with no radical changes.

Throughout this book, I have not been kind to the fashion industry because of its failure to design and manufacture clothing based on research rather than whim. Some readers may have gathered from my comments that the men of the fashion industry have concocted an insidious plot to take our money and make us a nation of slobs.

Although they have partially succeeded at the latter, this is not the result of any plot, but of their own stupidity; and they are in the long run only hurting themselves. The leisure suit, and the industry's campaign to make men believe it can replace the standard business suit, is ample proof. Substantial research by myself and another independent firm drew the same conclusions: Any office that allows the leisure suit as acceptable attire will eventually destroy the requirements for business suits. In any office where men can wear leisure suits, the relaxing of the rules will also mean that they can wear sweaters. If they can wear sweaters, after a time no men will wear suits—either business or leisure—and the suit manufacturers will be out of business. Yet the fashion people persist in this nonsense, even when research shows they could be destroying themselves.

DRESSING FOR THE COUNTRY CLUB

For many men, joining a country club is very important to their business as well as their social lives. One could almost write a book on the strata of country clubs in this country, but I will restrain myself and offer you some clothes-related hints instead.

In deciding which country club you should join, the look of the present membership can tell you a lot. You can almost decide whether the country club is "right" for you simply by estimating the percentage of members who either adhere to or break the sport-clothing rules in this book. If the biggest percentage of members break them, in all probability it's not the kind of country club that will do you any good if you're interested in moving upward in any traditional American industry.

In several studies I did for member clubs of the Club Managers Association of America, we found that in country clubs the stricter the official dress code (jacket required in the dining room, etc.), the "better" were the members in the Success-Ladder sense of the word.

Once you have chosen and joined a club, look carefully at the best-dressed and most-respected members in your age group, ask them where they buy their clothes, and give them the sincerest form of flattery, imitate them (without being too obvious). The reason for this rule? Country clubs tend to have individual personalities, just like people, and they develop their own dress habits and idiosyncrasies rather than standardized dress codes. As long as you associate your look with that of the best group, you will always be safe.

HOW TO PICK THE RIGHT FORMAL WEAR

Formal occasions require a combination of specific clothing that is separate and different from any other, and therefore absolutely useless for other occasions.

The gentleman's tuxedo is black, conservative and traditional. The gentleman who is not in show business should wear no other style or color. While some men *may* test well in other styles and other colors in some specific circumstances, all men test well in the traditional black.

Formal shirts should be elegant and simple, either in white or, occasionally, pale blue. Formal shirts require the use of studs and cuff links.

Studs and cuff links should be small, simple and as expensive as you can afford. Solid gold and gold and onyx are the most acceptable.

Tuxedos require black bow ties. There is absolutely no testable difference between the clip-on models and the tie-it-yourself models. None.

Formal wear requires the use of white or black suspenders, and most tuxedos require the use of a black cummerbund.

Formal wear requires the use of black, patent leather formal shoes and sheer black socks.

Although you will be told differently in almost any store that sells formal wear, the correct time to change to the white dinner jacket is when the weather demands it, and that depends on the area of the country. If it is hot, you wear white dinner jackets; if the weather is cool, you wear the black tuxedo. There are no dates that set apart these periods, and no stringent rules. The stringent rules exist only in the minds of those people who can't understand anything in the absence of stringent rules.

Happy rubber chicken and peas!

11.

HOW TO DRESS FOR SUCCESS WITH WOMEN

If you have read and started to follow the preceding advice in this book, you are definitely on the way to improving your business image and hopefully your chances for upward mobility.

But how's your sex life?

If you're counting for help on the clothes and combinations I have thus far recommended, it could probably stand improvement.

I wish I could report that a man's sexual image tagged right along with his business image, that the look of success after five o'clock is the same as the look of success before five o'clock. Unfortunately, the facts belie this. In American business, most people who make the important decisions in the lives of most men are other men. In American romance, the people who make the important decisions in the lives of most men are women. And most women's views of men's fashions are, as I've emphasized before, diametrically opposed to most men's views of men's fashions.

Unfortunately for the man who wants to dress for both business and romantic success, this dichotomy of taste requires two distinctly separate wardrobes, one for the office and one for the ladies. Hopefully, you can afford to cater to this double standard.

For the purposes of this discussion, when I refer to "most women," I mean most single women between the ages of eighteen and thirty-five. When referring to other types of women, I will so specify.

Since clothing is directly related to physical characteristics, I must first describe the type of man most women prefer. He is neither the Charles Atlas type nor the skinny fellow who always gets sand kicked in his face. He is young, well-muscled, relatively slim and relatively tall, with a thin waist, well-rounded buttocks, masculine hands and a masculine neck. The backs of the hands and neck are especially attractive to most women.

If you possess these lucky characteristics, it is to your advantage to show them off as best you can. If you are different, and most of us are, the trick is to camouflage your negative points.

For example, most women prefer a man with thin hips over a man with wider hips. If you take photographs of three men —one with thin hips dressed in tight clothing, one with wide hips dressed in loose clothing, and one with wide hips dressed in tight clothing—most women will prefer the man with the thin hips. But some women will prefer the man with wide hips who wears loose clothing. Virtually none will prefer the man with wide hips in tight clothing.

The reason is that most women have a great sense of appropriateness about clothes (even if that sense is largely misguided when it is applied to the business world) and they look upon a man with wide hips who wears tight clothing as too stupid to cover up his problem. When they dress themselves, women have been taking it from where it is and putting it where it ain't for years, and they expect (and have respect) for the man who does the same.

So display your sexy characteristics and cover your lack of them.

WHEN TO BARE YOUR CHEST

Most women like men in open shirts, but they expect this display of masculine chest to be confined to appropriate locations: at a bar, on the beach, at a sporting event, at his apartment or hers, but not on Fifth Avenue in New York. There, women find it tasteless and not very sexy.

Men who wear polo shirts as part of their casual attire should know that most women consider these shirts sexier if they are of darker colors than the pants or shorts they are worn with. When the shirt is not darker than the pants, it should be a solid color. For some reason, in casual shirting, women find solids sexier than patterns.

Most women do not find Bermuda or walking shorts sexy. In fact, they find them markedly unsexy, and much prefer the shorter tennis shorts.

HOW SLACKS SHOULD FIT TO PLEASE WOMEN

Slacks can fit a man in several different ways. The style that elicits the most favorable responses from women is the hip hugger, particularly if it is tight and worn by a man who has the figure to support it. Another type of pants that is attractive to women are those with high waistbands, which also tend to show off a man's hips and figure. Although women like a man's pants to be tight in the hips and on the upper legs, they are also attracted to pants that flare at the bottoms, probably because the flare increases the illusion of thin hips.

When I showed women a number of "costume" looks for men, the two that they found sexually most attractive and stimulating are the costume of the male flamenco dancer, and the tight jeans, open shirt and rough masculine look of the American cowboy. Obviously, no sane man is going to go into his neighborhood singles bar wearing a flamenco costume, but he can adopt the cut of such clothing to his more standard garb.

High heel shoes and boots make men stand differently,

which throws their hips into a different angle, and women find this attractive. If you have the choice, high-heel boots have a better connotation than high-heel shoes, which to some women imply femininity when worn by a man.

HOW SHIRTS AND SUITS SHOULD FIT

In standard dress shirts, women prefer tapered shirts on any man whose figure can support this style (see drawing below).

A "Body" Shirt
with Tapered Accent Lines,
Which Make the Chest
Look Larger and
the Waist Look Slimmer

Some tapered shirts—the Pierre Cardin is one example—are sewn in such a way that the seams add even more emphasis to the tapered look. If you do not have the figure for tapered shirts, again, do not wear them. Wear shirts that are loose, but not baggy or sloppy.

Most women prefer the European cut in suits, basically

because these tend to taper in at the waist and make for a highly shaped and thin-hipped look and also because European suits tend to be "with it" and up-to-date (see drawings on page 182). In addition, since women find the backs of men's hands and necks so attractive, high-fashion collars and the tendency to show more cuff add emphasis to these attractions. Women dislike any garment that bags or sags, and this includes overcoats, which should have the same tapered look as suits.

Although I've already warned you that excessive jewelry should never be worn to the office, women do find it attractive on men, so if you wish to wear it after hours, it is a sexual plus. But it's a minus unless it's tasteful. What's tasteful? Small and discreet and expensive is tasteful; large and gaudy and cheap is not.

WHAT WOMEN INFER FROM A MAN'S CLOTHES

When a woman sees a man who is not dressed well, she does not think that he isn't dressed well; she says to herself that he doesn't know how to dress well. And she then correlates his ability in dress with his other abilities, or lack thereof. She assumes that any man who knows how to put together tricky combinations is clever, and women like tricky combinations. As you will have gathered, I do not generally recommend putting patterns together; it is too difficult for most men to master well. But to attract women, it can work nicely.

With a plaid suit, it is possible to wear a wide-stripe shirt or an open-check shirt or a box-pattern shirt so long as the shirt pattern is smaller than the suit pattern and preferably in the same color. A muted paisley or small, neat pattern or tone-on-tone tie will compliment the look. Again, you must be adept at doing this, and knowing how to do it well is a gift.

With any of the striped suits I have recommended, you can wear a plaid or checked shirt with a club tie or plaid or paisley or bold print. If you can do it well, you will improve your attractiveness to women, but if you can't do it well, don't try.

Suits

European-Cut Suit

Standard American-Cut Suit

The best way to learn how to do it is to look at enough store windows. Whenever you see patterns on patterns that are effective, go in and buy both the shirt and tie together. Never take one without the other.

THE COLORS THAT ATTRACT WOMEN

In researching what colors women are attracted to in men's clothing, I found that they like dark, authoritative colors, even in sportswear, on the upper torso. Women are always attracted to "with-it" or "in" colors and to certain combinations, navy and maroon being the most prominent. Men who wear bright shirts with dark suits, and bright contrasting colors are considered clever. The only significance I found to be connected with the color red is that women feel that men wearing bright red ties are quite sexy.

Women definitely and always prefer men who are up-to-date; and in women's clothing, there are always in and out colors. If you keep abreast of women's in colors and adopt these for your own outfit, with discretion, most women will consider this quite clever.

HAIR STYLING AND COLOGNES HELP

Women are attracted to men who have their hair styled, to men who wear the most modern type of glasses—the thin, wire framed ones—and men with mustaches and long hair. They are completely turned off by men with dirty (or even dirty-looking) hair.

Women are attracted to certain smells; most of them say they like a man who "smells good." The men's colognes they found to be most appealing were somewhat surprising to me. They are Braggi, Bill Blass, Aramis, Canoe and even Old Spice. The more masculine smells that most men would think are the most appealing are not thought to be very sexy. In addition to wanting a man to smell good, most women are also attracted to men who smell like men after physical activity. If any cologne manufacturer can ever come up with a combination of both, he will have it made.

WHAT "SELF-CONFIDENCE" REALLY MEANS TO WOMEN

Most women will say that they are attracted to men who exude what they call "self-confidence," but what my follow-up research has shown is really more akin to arrogance.

In testing in singles bars on New York's upper East Side, I used two men who had tested equally sexy in the eyes of most women. When I asked the men to act in a self-confident or assured manner, the relationship between their demeanor and the way women were attracted to them was practically zero. Yet when I told the men to act arrogantly, they were far more successful in being judged sexy and attractive. I don't know the meaning of this, and am not sure I want to find out, but take it for what it's worth.

Women who are older than thirty-five react to just about the same stimulants as the younger women, with the exception that they are more attracted to slightly heavier men. They also tend to be less impressed with the European-cut suit, preferring men who wear more traditional, conservative suits, which is what they were brought up seeing at home. Generally, the older a woman is, the more apt she is to dislike men whose hair is styled.

When Don Juan was on his death bed, he was giving advice to a young man who wished to follow in his rather-to-be-envied footsteps. When it came to the discussion of the clothing the young man should wear to attract women, Don Juan told him simply to attract one woman and let her pick out his clothing. Thus clothed, the young man could then pick out all the other women he desired.

The advice is still quite sound. There isn't a woman in the world who wouldn't be flattered if asked to help choose a man's clothing, and almost all of them will choose garments that are sexually attractive on you. So let them. My only word of caution is to make sure that they pick out garments that are not going to be worn to the office, but only those you are buying specifically to make yourself attractive to women. Remember that the two definitely don't mix.

HOW TO DRESS FOR THE WOMEN IN YOUR OFFICE

Some men must dress for women in the office, but usually in order to be more authoritative rather than to be sexy. Most women who work in offices say that they like their bosses to dress with-it, mod, up-to-date in nice colors and clever combinations. They will say that they work harder for such men, but in every study I've ever done, I have found that the traditional look in clothing is far more effective for men in authority, if only one or several work under his supervision. If a man has a large group of women working for him, then it is essential that he dress up-to-date, that he keep the cut of clothes neat and sharp.

This does not mean that he should wear European-cut suits or bananas ties, but that he put his clothing together with some obvious care and that he make sure he knows at least what is going on in men's fashions and adhere to them somewhat. Women will have much more respect for him.

The man who has a great number of women working under him should wear dark, authoritative suits, dark blues, gray pin-stripes, and his suits should be very well tailored. He should make a particular effort to wear shirts and ties that are coordinated with his suits, and he should keep his personal appearance as neat as possible. If the man is much younger than the woman under him, he should dress even more conservatively than I have suggested. The one element of dress that every woman insists upon is executive-length socks, never ankle socks, which they find quite unpleasant. As do most men.

The same rules apply to the man who has a large number of women as colleagues. If he is neat and precise in his dress, his female co-workers will think more of him and be willing to help him more. Women do to men what they do to women. They apply the standards of their own sex to the other sex, either fairly or unfairly; and since being neat and well coordinated is a sign of being a decent, responsible woman to other women, they carry this attitude over to men.

Men who have women as bosses must adhere to a completely different set of rules. If a woman is going to make the basic or major decisions in your job life, then you must dress accordingly.

For several reasons, the woman who is a boss does not want a man working for her who is a threat or potential threat, and she will not promote any such man. Therefore, it is best for men working under women to wear lighter suits, never the darkest blue or darkest gray. He must keep his clothes up-to-date, wear fashionable shirts and ties, and avoid all pinstripes in all garments.

Men with women bosses should also not take too seriously any compliments that she makes on his dress. If her comments are negative, then he should change. But compliments are not going to get any man promoted. The man whom a female boss will promote is the one she thinks is most competent without being threatening, not the one she compliments as looking jazziest.

12.

FOR LAWYERS: HOW TO DRESS UP YOUR CASE AND WIN JUDGES AND JURIES

You may recall that when I became America's first wardrobe engineer, my initial clients were courtroom lawyers. Because of their diverse and important clothing needs and because they face constant and crucial problems concerning appearance— their own, their clients' and that of the juries before whom they must work—I have continued to advise a growing number of individual attorneys and law firms over the years.

Good courtroom lawyers are super salesmen and consummate actors, and they well realize that nonverbal forms of communication are frequently just as important (and sometimes more so) as the facts of a case. Clothing and appearance are hardly the only important nonverbal communicants, but they are the only ones within my province.

The rules for lawyers are much the same as for salesmen, but they must be broken down further and must be stated somewhat differently.

According to all my research, there are only two kinds of judges in America. Both come out of clubs. In the large urban areas, judges generally come from lower-middle-class backgrounds but have moved into the upper-middle class by virtue of their positions. Basically they come out of political clubs. In the case of rural or smalltown judges, the judges' daddies were usually judges and often their granddaddies were judges, too. They come out of the country club. The manner of dress should be almost the same before both groups, but some slight differences must be observed.

Before both groups, you should wear upper-middle-class clothing when you can. I say "when you can," because in some cases the attitude and makeup of the jury will be more important than the attitude of the judge; if so—and only each individual attorney can decide—clothing compensations must be made.

Before the urban judge, you should avoid the Ivy League tie. You should avoid any sign of ostentation. You should avoid any look that is with-it, chic or "in." Urban judges tend to be quite ticklish about their newfound socioeconomic positions, even if they've held them for some time, and often look upon anyone coming into their courtroom as a potential threat to them personally. Anyone who doesn't treat their courtrooms with respect, and that means anyone who dresses in a manner that *they* think is unbecoming, will be dealt with harshly. Their reactions may well be subconscious; no judge will ever tell you that he's ruling against you because of your smartass tie, but believe me, many of them will.

Although your clothing should be conservative in the urban courtroom, it should also be up-to-date. If four-and-a-half-inch ties are the predominant style in that locality, wear them, as long as they are in conservative and acceptable patterns and colors.

Rural or smalltown judges unconsciously observe much the same rules. The only difference is that you should never dress up-to-date before them. Rather, well-worn Brooks Brothers is the rule of the day, or whatever style is predominant with the local gentry.

Dressing for juries requires considerable acumen and practice because their makeup rarely fits textbook models. Once a jury has been chosen every lawyer should make a list of every person on that jury, according to those of the following factors that are most important. He should choose his clothing accordingly, just as he directs his case presentation accordingly.

The rarest jury in America today is the old-money jury, composed only or predominantly of the power or hereditary elite. With such juries, one should dress basically in the same clothing that one wears before the aforementioned judges. If the jury is in a rural area or small town, your clothing should be ultra conservative; if the jury is in or close to a large city, you can wear more up-to-date apparel, but every item and every detail of your clothing and your client's clothing must be immediately identifiable as upper-middle class if you expect to be accorded credibility.

Before grand juries in large cities, you are dealing with a slightly different social group. These tend to be self-made men and women without very well established backgrounds who have made it by virtue of intelligence and hard work. They consider themselves the backbone of the community and expect anyone appearing before them to affect a similar appearance if they are to be believed. With these jurors, the conservative dark blue suit is the most effective, either solid or with pinstripes, and the Ivy League tie must be avoided. The rep tie and solid shirt, which are staples of the male members' own wardrobes, are also effective.

In most suburban societies, you will find a varied but white population, and will therefore generally face a white jury with mixed socioeconomic backgrounds. In this area, I suggest dark blue suits, white shirts, rep ties and very structured appearances. This is the uniform that the lower-middle-class members of the jury expect. When dealing with lower-middle-class whites on a suburban jury, never wear a gray suit. I know this is the suit that most lawyers wear, but that's because they don't know not to.

According to a Burlington House study, most lower-middle-class whites buy suits for one social function: a funeral. Men at the lower socioeconomic levels are very unsure of themselves socially, even within their own group, and they have strict rules they live by. The dark blue suit is a symbol of important occasions and important people, and it is the one "good" suit that most lower-middle-class men have. If a lawyer comes into a courtroom wearing a gray suit and says to a jury made up of such men (or their wives) that he is their neighbor, their friend, one of them and that they should therefore believe him, his verbal approach may be perfect, but his visual approach is a lie.

They know that their friends do not wear gray suits on important occasions. If the lawyer wants to tell them, "I am in a position of authority, I am an expert, I know more than you and you should listen to me for that reason," then he may wear the gray suit, even with pinstripes and a vest, but he is taking a very serious risk because he may offend the jury by asserting his superiority.

Before the suburban black jury, the lawyer basically faces middle-class blacks who have worked themselves up out of the ghetto. They have made it in American society, and they expect to be treated as if they've made it. You should not wear the dark blue suit because to them it represents the old-line, anti-black establishment, which they neither like nor trust. Yet they display the typical, general middle-class prejudice of trusting only older members of the middle class.

The best suit to wear is a medium-range solid gray.

If you have an equal number of lower-middle-class whites and middle-class blacks on a suburban jury, dress for the blacks. The prejudice of the whites against gray will be less than the prejudice of the blacks against blue.

The white lawyer working before a black suburban jury is foolhardy if he attempts a "Hey, buddy, I'm one of you fellows" approach. It can't work. Therefore, he is much better off if he presents his case as an expert, and the gray suit is best, preferably combined with a light blue solid shirt and rep tie. Middle-class suburban blacks are quite status conscious, and they are offended by anyone who does not dress as they think he should.

All smalltown and rural juries have one major prejudice in

common: they detest the smartass big city slicker. The one essential rule before such juries is to wear nothing that indicates you are more sophisticated than they, nothing that indicates you are better than they, and absolutely nothing that they associate with big-city clothing. Whenever one of the richest and most successful lawyers in Chicago must try a case in southern Illinois, he drives down in a pickup truck and dresses very much as if he is more familiar with the truck than with a courtroom. I know a lawyer in New York who makes in excess of $300,000 a year, but whenever he must work on Long Island or an upstate farming area, he takes off his jacket, rolls up his sleeves, puts on the sloppiest tie he owns, and drives to court in his son's car.

The color prejudices of rural juries are exactly the same as the color prejudices detailed in Chapter 7, and the same geographic breakdown prevails.

Before rural juries, wearing dated clothing is an effective idea, as is a lawyer taking off his jacket, rolling up his sleeves and loosening his tie in the courtroom. Rural juries react negatively even to local lawyers who "put on airs." Anything one can do within reason to be as informal as possible and become regarded as one of the people is a positive move.

Because of their varied makeup, urban juries are by far the most difficult to dress for, but here are some basic rules.

If the jury is predominantly white and upper-middle class, you must wear upper-middle-class garments that are up-to-date and conservatively fashionable. If the jury is predominantly white and lower-middle class, their reactions will be virtually the same as those of the lower-middle-class suburban jury. So you should wear a dark blue suit, white shirt and very conservative tie. With an urban jury that is predominantly black but middle class, a medium-range gray suit, light blue solid shirt and rep tie work best.

Urban ghetto blacks on a jury changes all the rules dramatically. Since most of these blacks can be classified as antiestablishment, or leaning toward antiestablishment in their attitudes, you cannot wear standard courtroom garb successfully before them. (Women lawyers have much more innate credibility with ghetto blacks because women are not considered part of the establishment.) White male lawyers do better before ghetto black juries if they wear beards, if they are not too neat, if they display items that identify them as standing apart from the establishment and if they avoid any item of apparel that is authoritative. Young lawyers will do better before ghetto black juries; age in a white lawyer is an automatic negative with most blacks.

The real problem with urban juries is that the judge is almost always white and upper-middle-class while the jury seldom is, and is mixed at best. The lawyer in such cases must decide where his most critical problems are and dress to meet them. If he decides to dress for the jury, though, he should at least make a conscious attempt not to turn off the judge.

Minority lawyers working before judges should follow the same rules recommended for white lawyers. Minority lawyers working before minority juries should wear establishment clothing that exudes success. The best garb for the minority lawyer in a courtroom, assuming that he knows nothing about the judge or jury, is a dark pinstripe suit with vest, a white shirt and a conservative tie. The look communicates to whites that the lawyer is no threat, and it says to blacks, "Look at me, I have made it," which is the most positive possible message.

In general, all lawyers should advise their clients to dress in ways similar to the lawyer's own garb in the above situations. Some subtleties can offer additional help. The most innocent look is the young look, and the younger a client can look, the better off he is. Close-cropped hair, closely shaven—any detail of appearance that Hollywood has conditioned people to equate with angelic qualities works wonders.

If you have a client with a beard or mustache, no matter who is on the jury or who the judge is, make him cut them off. Have him dress as conservatively as possible, in a dark suit, white shirt and conservative tie. As strange as it may seem, the look of innocence crosses all racial, age, socioeconomic and sex lines.

For Lawyers: How to Dress Up Your Case

Carefully planned clothing can provide an effective boost for any client. For example, when your client is on the stand and *you* are examining him to get your version of the story across, put him in a very soft gray suit (authoritative but not offensive), a solid-white or pale blue shirt and a light gray and blue tie, something with large patterns or perhaps a solid color. Your goal is to have the client look calm and to have the jury remember what he says. Dressed in such an easy-to-look-at combination, the jury can look at him for a full day and remember a great deal of what he says.

When the prosecutor or attorney for the other side is questioning him, if possible, put him a very dark blue suit, a crisp white shirt and a bright red tie, preferably with a difficult-to-look-at but still elegant pattern. Put a bright red handkerchief in his breast pocket. This combination will make it quite difficult for the jury to look at him, and the less they look at him the less they will remember of what he says.

If he's being questioned by your side and wears glasses, have him remove them before taking the stand; if being questioned by the other side, have him wear them.

A week and a half later, when the jury is deliberating they will remember far more of what he said in his easy-to-look-at appearance than in his difficult-to-look-at appearance.

If you are representing a client who is accused of having power and misusing it in any kind of so-called white-collar crime, diminish his look of authority by having him wear a pale beige suit, a pale shirt (not light blue) and a pale tie. This combination suggests to a jury that this is not really a man of authority and raises the question of how he could have misused what he obviously doesn't have.

If you are defending one of the men in a mass trial, it is very often to your advantage to disassociate him from the other defendants. If this is the case, you should dress differently from all the other lawyers, even if it means appearing somewhat outlandish, and the client should dress differently from the other defendants. The visual separation will definitely help.

193

In a case on which I was consulted, involving three men accused of corporate shenanigans, my client took my advice and dressed much differently from the other two. He was found innocent while the others were found guilty. On the facts presented, one of the other two was clearly innocent, but he looked so much like the third man who was clearly guilty that the jury lumped them together in their verdict. Any experienced lawyer can cite many cases when clients were found guilty simply because they dressed incorrectly.

In addition to using clothing as a courtroom tool for themselves, clothes-conscious lawyers can tell much about prospective jurors merely from their appearance. When I was researching this aspect of trial work, I placed all potential jurors into three categories: strongly antiestablishment; neutral, but tending toward prejudice against large organizations; and proestablishment. About 28 percent of the population is composed of strongly antiestablishment people; approximately 12 percent is composed of strongly proestablishment people; and approximately 60 percent are neutral. But if the neutral people are sitting on a case involving a corporation against an individual, no matter what the nature of the case is, they will tend automatically to favor the individual.

In any jury selection, approximately 60 percent of the people, regardless of their category, will *attempt* to be fair, while the remaining 40 percent will vote, to a certain extent, based on preconceived prejudices. Any lawyer must decide, based on any individual case, which groups are in his best interest to sit on the jury, and which are in his worst interests, and strike them accordingly. (Obviously, in all my advice to lawyers, I am well aware that there are many factors in addition to clothing that affect decisions, but my advice is limited to appearance since that is what I know.)

People who are openly antiestablishment generally identify themselves quite readily. Any woman who is disheveled, wears hippie or bohemian attire, has an austere look with her hair tied back in a tight bun, affects mannish dress or rather unfeminine dress components, goes braless, or who either verbally or by dress identifies herself as a proponent of women's liberation should definitely be regarded as an antiestablishment type. Women over thirty who wear dark glasses in a courtroom would fall into the same category, although women who are younger than thirty usually do this only because they think it's in.

Obviously, an antiestablishment look varies from community to community, which individual lawyers must take into consideration. In New York City, for example, there are many more acceptable establishment looks than there are in Kansas City.

Any man anywhere who wears shoulder-length hair or beads or bracelets is antiestablishment. Afros on blacks tend to indicate the same attitude. Men who wear unusual color combinations tend to be antiestablishment. Normally, this would mean bright color combinations or bright colors in individual garments—orange shirts, red jackets, green and yellow and purple ties—but unusual combinations can also be mixed into a normally conservative look. For example, if a man wears a pair of black pants, a dark blue jacket, a green pinstripe shirt and a black tie, he does give off a conservative impression, but the combination is unusual enough to assume that the man is probably antiestablishment.

Another typically antiestablishment person is the one who dresses down for jury duty, someone who dresses obviously poorer than he would in everyday life. These people treat jury duty as a lark, and act and dress as if they're going to work in the yard or rake leaves. They may be top executives who wear scruffy pants and unshined shoes. One must be careful to determine a prospective juror's occupation because an executive who dresses this way is dressing down, but a cabdriver does it out of necessity and habit and is not dressing down.

Men whose educational levels are equivalent to those of most executives—college level or above—but whose appearances would exclude them from executive ranks, tend to be antiestablishment. This group includes college graduates with beards, who wear only lower-middle-class clothing, or whose hair length would be unacceptable in a corporate job.

White-middle-class men who wear either orange or purple in any obtrusive way and men who wear shirts or ties with wild patterns tend to be antiestablishment. This is not true of many blacks and men of Spanish origin, who may wear wilder patterns and colors as a matter of custom.

The strongest proestablishment types are executives who look the part in the courtroom. They come to court dressed in the same clothes they would wear to work, standard business suits, acceptable shirts and ties. Next comes lower-middle-class men who do not wear shirts and ties in their daily lives— bartenders, truck drivers, cab drivers—but who do dress up for jury duty. They do so because they believe jury service is an important obligation.

Men who are extremely precise—with every hair in place, a perfectly knotted tie, impeccably fitting clothes—also tend to be proestablishment, as do men who seem to look old-fashioned. By this I do not mean that their clothing is dated, only that it is extremely conservative. Such men wear narrow-lapeled suits, narrow ties, button-down shirts and lace shoes. Also tending to be proestablishment are men who dress for jury duty just as they dress for work, regardless of their occupations, and men who wear traditional patterns, even if these patterns are on rather casual clothes.

Because of the extreme variety of acceptable women's clothing, it is quite difficult to identify proestablishment women by appearance alone. Women who dress conservatively tend to be proestablishment, and even though this is the only reasonable indicator I have been able to isolate, it is not always accurate.

Once a potential juror has been placed in one of the above categories by the lawyer, it is time to begin more extensive questioning of the individual to determine his propensity to either help or hurt a particular case. Veteran trial lawyers are well aware that some potential jurors will lie in answer to questions, some to get on cases, some to get off them, and some for countless other reasons.

For Lawyers: How to Dress Up Your Case

Although I do not pretend I can spot any liar in a courtroom merely by appearance, in my many years of advising and consulting with lawyers, I have come up with several identifiable types who tend to lie and should be questioned and challenged far more attentively than most other people.

The first type, and the easiest to spot, are people—both men and women—who have no self-image, no self-esteem. They wear clothes that obviously do not fit, that are mismatched; their hair is not combed; their shoes may be scuffed and unshined—not because of economic necessity, but because they do not care. In questioning anyone who falls into this pattern, it is often wise to ask questions already asked by the opposing attorney to check for discrepancies. This type of person tends to tell each attorney what he thinks that attorney wants to hear, and although he's not telling a deliberate lie—he's lying to himself as much as to the lawyer—the end result remains the same: He is a liar.

The second type is the habitual liar, the person who lies all the time and to whom lying is just as natural as wearing a coat in winter. This type of person uses lying as part of his everyday weaponry in dealing with the world and generally lies visually as well as verbally. Men or women who dress as if they are in an age group other than their own—a forty-five-year-old woman dressed like a teeny bopper, a twenty-five-year-old man who dresses as if he were sixty—definitely fit into this category. People who dress in contrast to their socioeconomic status— professional men who dress as if they are not, plumbers who dress like stockbrokers (not the plumber who dresses up for court, putting on a shirt and tie, but the plumber who is wearing all the correct upper-middle-class symbols)—these people are lying to themselves about who they are, and they are very likely to lie to you.

The only exception to this rule is young people. Whether they are or are not, many of them look at themselves as being outside the establishment and they dress accordingly. They are generally not lying to themselves, but really are trying to be honest with themselves, and they will generally be honest with you.

The easiest visually-detectable liar is the job description liar. If a man is earning his living as an accountant, he is a part of the establishment whether he knows it or not and whether he admits it or not. If he dresses or acts or has his hair cut in any way that says he is not an accountant, then he is putting on the world and putting on himself. Either way, he is more likely to be untruthful than the accountant who looks, acts and dresses like an accountant. The same is true of truckdrivers, doctors, of almost any group.

All of the preceding guidelines are no more than that. Every lawyer must take into consideration the tremendous variations that can occur, the amount of personal judgment that is required on the spot and use the guidelines accordingly.

13.

HOW TO DRESS UP YOUR OFFICE FOR SUCCESS

Obviously, professional qualifications are important for lawyers, doctors, architects and others who are in business for themselves, including wardrobe consultants. But so are appearances, and the only appearance that will help such men is the appearance of success, prestige and power. I hope that I have by now established how importantly clothing contributes to this look of success. Another significant element in this look of success that can be controlled is the physical setup of your office.

Unfortunately, most corporate executives have little control over the look of their offices because the office arrangement, furniture and decor are usually controlled by the companies for which they work, at least to a considerable extent. Such control, however, is absolutely crucial to any man who must bring in business, who must bring in clients or patients from the outside, and especially professionals in business for themselves. Corporate executives would be well advised to follow as many of my research-based tips as their managements will permit.

The impression that anyone from the outside will have of any man will depend in no small measure on the setting in which he sees that man functioning—his office. Men have realized for years that offices are important. But most have not sought to systematize their concern, to make their offices yield the ultimate benefits possible.

The people who sell office furniture are much too concerned with selling the products they have been given to sell than with selling power. They are much more interested in selling something new rather than something useful. There are some decorators who are wizards at office arrangement, furnishing and decor, but they are few and very expensive.

HOW TO MAKE IT BIG

Like successful clothing, the successful office exudes the qualities of the upper-middle class. It is (or looks) spacious and uncrowded. It is rich. It is well kept. It is tasteful. It is impressive. It is comfortable. It is private.

The most important aspect of any office is size; it should be as large as possible. Obviously there are financial limitations attached to this advice, but if you have a section consisting of several offices, as most professional men do, and you must skimp, be sure to skimp somewhere other than on your personal office.

About as important as your office's size and richness is its address. The best addresses are generally the most expensive, and you should have, regardless of the city you work in, the most prestigious address you can afford. This is even more important if some of your clients come from a distance. For years, most of my clients have been from New York, and I maintained an office on West 55th Street, right off Fifth Avenue. Knowledgeable New Yorkers know that this is a highly respectable location, but to the executive from Kansas City or the banker from Amarillo who may be considering my services, West 55th Street might at first suggest West 55th Street off Eighth Avenue where his best friend was mugged returning from the theater last year. So now, since more and more of my clients and prospective clients are from areas away from New York, I am moving to a Fifth Avenue office. To any man I want as a client, Fifth Avenue suggests prestige and substance. Any man to whom it doesn't say that, I can't help much anyway.

An office with a window or windows is better than an office without. An office with a window and a beautiful view is the best you can come by. If the view through your window is of an air shaft or similar atrocity, be very sure to keep your window covered.

The ideal office has two well-defined and separate areas: one in which the central object is your desk; and the other an informal conversation area, with a couch and/or chairs in a comfortable grouping. The best office for such an arrangement is L-shaped, but that is quite difficult to come by unless you have the money and ability to rearrange walls (see drawing on page 202).

TOP PRIORITY: THE DESK

After you have chosen your office, the most essential piece of furniture, and it should be chosen first, is your desk. The desk should be as large as possible without crowding or dwarfing the office. A desk that overpowers the space into which it is put creates a strongly negative impression. Regardless of its style, a desk should be functional for your needs and work habits. It should be wood or have the look of wood and should be as expensive as you can afford. All types of metal desks should be generally avoided; they do not look as if they belong to a man of substance and power.

The next item to acquire is your desk chair. In most cases, the best chair is a large one that comes up to the back of the head. It should be a standard office chair, various styles of which will blend with any decor from antique to ultramodern. The only man who should avoid the large chair is the very small man. He should choose a chair proportional to his size because a large chair will make him look even smaller.

In front of your desk should be two comfortable chairs for

Large Office

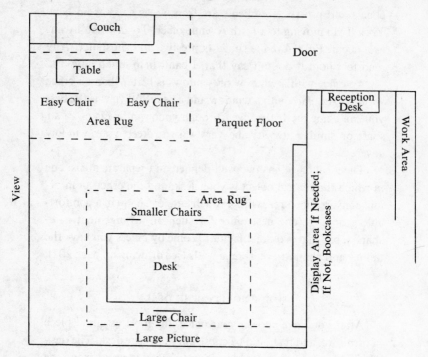

Couch

Door

Table

Easy Chair   Easy Chair

Area Rug   Parquet Floor

Reception Desk

Work Area

View

Smaller Chairs   Area Rug

Desk

Display Area If Needed; If Not, Bookcases

Large Chair

Large Picture

Small Office

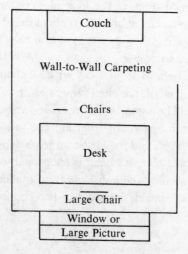

Couch

Wall-to-Wall Carpeting

— Chairs —

Desk

Large Chair

Window or
Large Picture

visitors. They should be of good quality, in either leather or Naugahyde, preferably matching your desk chair. The most acceptable colors for desk and visitor's chairs are deep maroon, deep green, a dark, rich brown or natural leather. The most common color that is manufactured and sought after is black, but it is not as effective as the above colors because they give off a much richer look.

WHERE VISITORS SHOULD SIT

Always place visitors' chairs in front of your desk, never on the sides. Somehow, when a visitor moves up to the side of your desk, he invades your area of privacy and cuts down on your authority in dealing with him. Sitting on the side is not as psychologically comfortable for him nor as effective for you. Keep the chairs in front of the desk.

Depending on the space available for your second area, you should at least have a couch (it can be small if necessary) and a coffee-type table that fits in with the rest of the room's decor. If you have the space, add two comfortable, living room-type chairs. If you have an exceptionally large office, and if your work requires it, you might also add a third area in which you would place a small work or conference table with chairs around it. The best example I've ever seen of this was an antique table with matching antique chairs; it gave the powerful impression of a small board room in the office.

The only other items of furniture that are completely acceptable in most offices are bookcases, credenzas and filing cabinets. But if at all possible, you should keep your filing cabinets in your secretary's office or in some other area. Important men just do not have obtrusive filing cabinets in their offices.

HOW TO HIDE PAPERS

If you are in a type of business that requires you to have a lot of papers in your office, I suggest that you keep them on top of a credenza behind your desk rather than on your desk. A clean, neat, uncluttered desk is absolutely essential to a spacious, uncrowded-looking office, and to any man of prestige and power.

Bookcases are both useful and impressive, so long as they contain useful or relevant or impressive items—business or reference books, leather-bound first editions, small art works, perhaps antique items related to your business, a stereo set if you are in the music business, small personal collections such as scrimshaw, etc. But don't go overboard with these items. I have been in offices filled with globes, which is fine for men in worldwide businesses, but somewhat excessive for accountants. The one item of furniture that should never be present or visible in any office is a bar; many men will object to it.

Before buying any item of furniture for an office, make a scale drawing of the room and of the furniture you want. If it looks spacious and uncrowded, fine; if anything makes the office look crowded, do not buy it. If you already have it, throw it out. It is far more important that an office look open than that it contain any particular item.

HOW TO GET THE MOST OUT OF FLOOR COVERING

After acquiring the necessary and appropriate furniture, choose a floor covering. The best flooring is parquet covered with several area rugs delineating and separating the different areas of the office. The next best, particularly if your office is too small to handle several rugs, is parquet flooring covered with a room-size rug that leaves about a twelve-inch border of wood showing around the room. The wood must be finished properly, and the quality of the rugs is quite important. Unless your office is ultramodern, then the richest, most expensive oriental rugs you can afford are perfect for offices. They are warm, colorful and distinguished.

If you do not have or cannot install good wooden flooring, then choose wall-to-wall carpeting. There is really no other solution in the offices of important men. Tile or inlaid linoleum are strong negatives and should never be used. If you do have wood, never leave it bare; bare wood is too cold and makes sounds echo too loudly.

Whatever type of carpeting you have, keep it clean. Most decorators choose pale rugs, and most executives never see to keeping them clean or replacing them when necessary. Dirty or shabby rugs are not proper symbols for the offices of successful men.

BEST WALLS, CEILINGS AND COLORS

Having purchased your furniture and covered your floors, you are ready to cover your walls. If your office is small, white walls will make it look more spacious. If the ceiling is low, the lighter the color it is painted, the higher it will look. If the ceiling is too high for the size of the office, you might make the walls white and the ceiling pale blue, which will seem to bring it down. If any one wall of the office seems too distant from the rest of the office, painting it a darker color than the other walls will help; adding paintings or bookcases to such a wall will also help.

Assuming that the office is of a suitable size, off-white or eggshell or very light beige—which are all the same color, really, but paint manufacturers have their own names—is the best wall coloring for a man's office. The only other completely suitable color is pale blue. All others will tend to get you into varying kinds of psychological trouble.

If you are going to use wallpaper, the textured types are best for a man's office. There are excellent grasscloths, woven bamboos and woodish varieties that offer richness, depth and substance to an office.

Some men, because of their businesses, must keep bulletin boards, charts, graphs or plans on their walls. If you must, try to keep them in an unobtrusive a place as possible, preferably on the wall with the entrance into the office, never behind you.

HOW TO "FRAME" YOURSELF FOR MAXIMUM AUTHORITY

In the ideal office, the desk acts like a throne, giving you power over those who come in. They should be impressed with your importance and authority. The best way to create this impression by instant visual impact is to position your desk and yourself within a frame that automatically turns you into its central element. The best elements to create such a frame are either a window or pictures directly behind the desk. The best frame is an open window with a beautiful view. If you have such a view, use it as the central frame behind your desk. Although most decorators ignore such considerations, if one has a view of constant colors (not seasonal ones such as green trees), and these colors are followed through in the office, the dimensions of the office will seem to be extended.

If you do not have, or are unable to position your desk in front of the window, paintings will accomplish the same effect. You must decide what painting, how large and how many, but regardless of these decisions the painting or paintings should be symmetrically positioned directly behind the desk, and not appear off-center or askew.

HOW TO SPOIL A WELL-DESIGNED OFFICE

Many men hire decorators to do their offices, and the decorators do magnificent jobs with all the major items. But after the decorator is gone, many a man then decides to personalize the office with a clutter of paraphenalia on his desk and doodads around the room. Don't make those mistakes. Keep on your desk only what you absolutely need there, nothing else. And don't clutter the room with extraneous doodads or junk. When the office is finished, and ready for you to work in it, to see clients or patients in it, it should be clean, clear, spacious and sparsely decorated with only tasteful elements, if you wish it to be effective.

Some decorators and some men might disagree with my advice, but just keep in mind one thing. I am not interested that a man have a beautiful office (although there is no reason why he can't and still adhere to my rules); I am interested that a man choose and furnish and decorate his office as a functional tool, as a symbol of power and importance so that he may better perform his job and increase his income.

The best general look and feel of an office is the look of wood and leather. A wooden desk, wooden bookcases, wooden paneling, wooden arms on chairs all look rich and luxurious and impressive. The modern look of chrome and steel and glass is also acceptable, but the man who chooses such a look must make up his mind that the office decor and furniture must be changed every few years. Modern offices, because of their stark lines and sharp contrasts, tend to become boring very quickly, both to the inhabitant and his frequent visitors, and modern furniture tends to date very quickly.

The man whose business absolutely requires the keeping of files in his personal office should consider using a modern office, if only because modern filing cabinets tend to be rather attractive, while old-fashioned ones look terrible. The man with money and an imaginative decorator can also come up with some creative and unobtrusive places and furniture in which to keep files, but this gets quite expensive, and the modern look is far easier on the wallet for most men.

HOW TO TEST THE EFFECTIVENESS OF YOUR OFFICE

A very simple way to test the effectiveness of your office is to photograph it from the entrance door and also to photograph (from the same perspective) the offices of several friends who work in the same profession. Then show the pictures to strangers and ask them to rate the importance of the men, only in terms of their offices. You'll get a pretty good idea of where your office stands comparatively.

In addition to your own personal office, you must also be concerned with your secretary's office or area. Four general rules apply for a secretary's office:

1. It should be tied into the boss's office in some way, usually

by proximity, so that there is no confusion as to whose secretary she is.

2. Although it should be tied in, it should be distinctly different from that of the boss. If it is a miniature copy of his office, this would cut down on his authority. The best way to achieve this distinction is to change the color of the carpet or the type of floor covering as you move from one area to the other.

3. The secretary's office should be a separate, defined area, not just a space that is encroached upon by general office traffic. It must be arranged so that the secretary has a sense of territorial domain. This increases her sense of power and authority, and greatly boosts her effectiveness.

4. A secretary should face so as to look parallel to her boss's door, never away from it or into it.

AND HOW DOES YOUR SECRETARY DRESS?

Very definitely related to the authoritative look of any office is the dress of a man's secretary. This is an element that is very delicate and often impossible to control—particularly since most secretaries work for less than munificent salaries and don't like their tastes and private lives encroached upon. Still the more ladylike, dignified, prestigious and efficient she looks, the better impression she will make on all visitors, and the better they will think of you.

If you're in any business that must attract clients, never forget that they are your most precious assets; that without them, you're out of business. You must make them comfortable and make them believe you are important at all times, and this includes the time they spend in your waiting room. It's the first part of your offices that they see, and will leave a distinct impression on them. Your chairs or couches should be comfortable and substantial; they should be clean and pleasantly arranged.

The waiting room, like all the rest of your office, must immediately spell "upper-middle class" to every visitor. Good wood, good leather or good upholstered furniture will always accomplish this; modern furniture sometimes will not, and you must be careful in its use. Good rugs or good carpeting will help. A decorator look will help, although this is not a foolproof concept because not all decorators can produce a decorator look.

Tasteful art work, whether paintings, prints or sculpture, give an upper-middle-class impression. The easiest (and one of the most effective) ways to create an upper-middle-class look in a waiting room is the right choice of magazines. Any combination of *Time, Newsweek, U.S. News and World Report* and the major business magazines—*Fortune, Forbes, Business Week, Barron's, Dun's Review*—plus whatever prestigious speciality or general interest magazines are relevant to you or your clients all make a good and lasting impression, provided they are always the latest issues and not torn and tattered.

14.

A SPECIAL WORD FOR THE PROFESSIONAL MAN

Once you master upper-middle-class dress, the differences in your effectiveness are only a matter of degree. But here are some specific rules for those men who are in business for themselves and must attract and keep clients or patients in order to stay in business.

Upper-middle-class clothing attracts upper-middle-class clients, and neutral clothing attracts neutral clients (those who may belong to any class but need and can afford your services). Typically, neutral clothing consists of a solid dark blue suit, white shirt and any conservative tie, preferably the rep. Acceptable upper-middle-class garments are those adequately described in the rest of the book.

If your job requires that you represent yourself as an expert, even to the lower-middle class, you should wear upper-middle-class garments. If you must sell yourself to industry as an expert, you must dress to look relevant to your field. An artist should not look like a stockbroker and a stockbroker should not look like an accountant.

A Special Word for the Professional Man

Once you have achieved the look of your field, you must look as if you are successful at it. If you're a stockbroker, you will do much better wearing a $400 suit and a $30 tie than you will if you wear anything less. The artist or creative type may never wear anything but jeans and sweaters, but he should select only those that are well-tailored, obviously expensive and in excellent taste.

If every man who must attract clients were to dress every day so he looks at least as successful, as conservative and as well turned out as any client he is ever likely to meet, he will dramatically improve his success. (I have done this for consulting firms who reimbursed their staff consultants for the clothing I chose for them, and these investments proved to be extremely profitable.)

Medical men fall into a very unusual category, and although most medical men couldn't be less concerned with their appearance, they should be. There are five basic uniforms that medical men wear—let me start with the worst. The upper-middle-class suit is absolutely taboo; most people object to a doctor looking like a successful businessman. Next comes the neutral suit—the dark blue solid or, in the Midwest, some shades of brown. The neutral suit is basically classless, and a doctor can wear it, but I advise against it. Many doctors wear conservative sport jackets and slacks as a matter of course, and of all "street clothing," this is probably the best combination, acceptable for all purposes other than extremely serious consultations.

The doctor's hospital all-whites, worn without a shirt and tie, are the next-to-best thing he can wear while working. It is a high authority outfit. But the best outfit, and the one that is the easiest to affect, is slacks worn with an upper-middle-class shirt and upper-middle-class tie and white doctor's jacket. This look conveys that the doctor is a member of an elite group. It definitely identifies him as a doctor and, as much as appearance can accomplish this, makes whatever he says and does seem all but infallible.

For men on the periphery of medicine—chiropractors,

podiatrists, optometrists, etc., whose specialties are often mis-understood and sometimes held in low esteem—the shirt, tie and white jacket can improve their credibility tremendously and should become their standard wardrobe.

15.

HOW TO USE CLOTHING TO BOOST THE CORPORATE IMAGE

About six months ago, a new client from the Midwest came to see me. All I knew about him was that he was a banker and had contracted for my services for one day. He arrived in my office at 10:00 o'clock that morning, and said that he'd like personal advice on his clothing. Would I go shopping with him?

After about an hour of questioning him about his needs, we headed for Fifth Avenue, and by lunchtime we had purchased him several suits. We decided to have lunch, and buy matching shirts and ties later in the day.

Over lunch, he told me that when he had called me to arrange for my time, he really wasn't thinking of clothing for himself (that was his wife's idea), but that he wanted to talk with me about uniforms for his bank. Since the time of his call to me he had solved that problem, he said, and so he had decided to use my time for himself. Since a large percentage of my corporate business is devoted to consulting about uniforms, I inquired how he had solved his problem.

He showed me a copy of a magazine called *Midwestern Banker* containing an article entitled "Careful Research Precedes Bank's Career Apparel Decision." The article stated that a bank had put together a committee of three branch department administrators, the manager of the main office, the bank's public relations officer and two marketing officers to choose their uniforms. Three of the individuals were women, and the article crowed about how wonderfully successful this "careful research" approach had been.

The uniforms were pictured in the article, and I could tell from a glance that they hadn't been all that successful, but I let that ride for several reasons. Instead, I went into a bit of a game that I often play. I told him that I didn't agree with the committee approach, but that it was being used by many companies to make important decisions, and that one of the banks with which I was associated actually used it to decide any number of important banking procedures, which I told my new client about.

About halfway through my recitation he stopped me and said that this approach was a foolish way to go about really important banking decisions, that they required coordination and a great deal of skill. As he wound himself up, without my saying anything, he gradually got the message that I wanted him to get—that he was making the same mistake with uniforms that he was now criticizing the other bank for making.

He stopped his monologue and rather sheepishly asked me what he should do.

THREE REVEALING QUESTIONS ABOUT COLORS

As a test, I asked him to call the chairman of his uniform committee and ask him the following three questions:

1. In Detroit (the bank's location) as well as the northern Midwest, one particular shade of green is believed by most citizens to be worn by thieves. Did the chairman know what that shade was? It later turned out that he did not.

2. Did he know what upper-middle-class colors were? He did not, although three of the bank's branches were in exclusively upper-middle-class areas.

3. Were the men's and women's uniforms all the same color, and should they be? He said of course.

At that point, I had signed up another uniform consulting contract.

WHERE UNIFORMS GO WRONG

American industry has very little idea what a proper corporate image is, and knows even less about how to achieve it. I start with uniforms, because it is important, and it is probably the area of operations where the most mistakes are made. Corporate executives appoint committees or individuals who have absolutely no background or experience in this field and assume that through osmosis and the brilliance of the uniform companies, they are going to learn how to choose a corporate look for their employees that may appear undramatic but is actually extremely complicated to achieve. This is not at all the way it works in reality.

Take color, for example. Nine times out of ten, the color of uniforms is determined, not by the needs of the corporation, but by the socioeconomic backgrounds of the employees choosing the uniforms. People are conditioned to certain shades of color. If we are talking about a bank, where employees usually come from lower-middle-class backgrounds, and that bank is in an exclusively upper-middle-class neighborhood, then the lower-middle-class colors chosen by the employees (and perfectly acceptable to them) would not stimulate great trust and faith from the bank's customers, although the customers would probably not be able to verbalize their negative reactions.

SIX RULES FOR CHOOSING UNIFORMS

As I say, it's a complicated business, so let me give you a few rules for the unfortunate executive who gets stuck with a job he's really not qualified to do without some briefing:

1. Only buy from a well-established uniform company. Even

then you must be careful; your interests are not necessarily theirs.

2. Try to choose stock uniforms, since you cannot predict how the details of custom-made garments will come off.

3. Get some guarantee that the uniform fabric is being manufactured by a major mill. Get an airtight written guarantee that the material will be produced continually for years to come, so that you can get the same uniform five years from now if you are happy with it.

4. Hire an outside firm to have the standard wear research done on the uniform before buying. There should be comparative statistics so you can evaluate the research.

5. Insist on speaking to corporate executives at other companies who have purchased identical uniforms. Ideally, they would be in a similar climatic area to yours.

6. Insure that the uniform company has a true tailoring service in your area—not just some local tailor they hired to get your contract—and speak to someone who has used that tailoring service.

With only those rules in mind, anyone should be able to buy uniforms for a corporation and not get burned too badly. But the real task comes long before you ever start talking to the uniform company. Your first question is not what uniform you need, but whether you need uniforms at all. What is the function of a uniform in the first place?

WHY UNIFORMS?

The most important function of a uniform is to add authority to the person wearing it. Of all the businesses in the country, the airlines understand this best. Their stewardesses—who, regardless of training and expertise in airline safety, spend most of their time as (forgive me, women!) waitresses in the sky—wear uniforms. Although bowing to fashion (which dovetails with the "hostess" part of their jobs), most stewardess uniforms are reasonably authoritative, and immediately identify the women as authority figures in times of emergency.

The uniforms of the pilot, co-pilot and navigator are in no way fashionable. Never. But their black or navy uniforms, white shirts and black or navy ties are the supreme authority uniforms. They exude power, competence and authority. They also reassure by conveying the soothing message: "We will take care of you."

The separation of the two distinct looks is important. It would be quite simple to have the stewardesses wear uniforms that are female copies of the pilot's uniforms (and in the earlier years of commercial flight, when great fear was prevalent among passengers, the stewardesses' uniforms were much more severe and formal), but while this would increase the stewardesses' authority, it would decrease that of the pilot through association. It would also decrease the friendly, feminine image of the stewardesses as hostesses, and make them much too formal and powerful for that part of their jobs. In practice, the uniform of each crew member today defines his image and establishes his function perfectly.

A GUARD CAN'T LOOK LIKE A NOBODY

The function of the uniform must also mesh with the people whom the wearer of that uniform must deal with. Several years ago, I was dressing the sales force of an Oregon manufacturer who owned two plants. While talking in the office one day, he asked if I could do anything to help him stop employee thievery. He said that his guards wore uniforms, because he knew this added to their authority, but he must not be doing something right, because the volume of theft was so high. I asked him to let me see the uniforms, and he said, "Okay, I'll send one of the guards out for a sandwich."

He made a call and, a few minutes later, a guard wearing a baggy blue uniform came in, bearing sandwiches and coffee.

When the guard had left, I said, "That's your problem."

He didn't know what I meant, and I went on to explain, "You dress your guards to look like nobodies who should be sent for coffee; you do send them for coffee; and everyone else in the plant, even if they don't send him, looks upon a guard as someone who could and should be sent. He couldn't protect anything because of his image; he's not a guard but a gofer and everyone knows it."

After spending several days around the plant, I came up with the following approach. We changed the guards' title to "security officer"; we took away their poorly shaped "uniform" uniforms and gave them well-tailored, upper-middle-class, conservative suits, shirts and ties; and we prohibited them from running errands. Within six months, employee thievery was cut in half.

By solving one problem, however, I had created another. Since the guards were now wearing suits and ties, they were not identifiable to outsiders, so burglaries at night increased. Therefore, we had to establish two distinctly separate uniforms, leaving the day men in their suits, but changing the night men into uniforms that were as close as we could come to those of the local police. (Since his two factories were separated by several hundred miles and the uniforms of the police in each locality differed, we had to have separate uniforms for the night guards at each factory.) Once these changes were completed, thievery in the two plants, from both inside and outside, was significantly diminished. So the function of uniforms depends much more on the people the wearer must deal with (or influence) than on his actual job.

As already mentioned, if the largest percentage of people any uniformed person must deal with and influence are of the upper-middle class, then the uniform absolutely must use only the upper-middle-class colors outlined in previous chapters of this book.

The geography and ethnic background of your customers or clientele can further be instrumental in the success of any uniform. For example, while one particular shade of green indicates to the greatest percentage of the population in Detroit that the wearer is a thief, dark blue jackets evoked a negative response in a ghetto in New York City. If you had a bank in either of those areas, those colors in your uniforms would not enhance the bank's image, and could conceivably hurt it. Unfortunately, these local prejudices—which could wreak havoc with the uniforms of national or multinational corporations—cannot be determined without specific research.

WHO SHOULD WEAR A UNIFORM—AND WHO SHOULDN'T

In deciding on uniforms, you are always faced with the problem of who should wear them and how far they should be extended in the company. Say that you own a bank (since banks must always deal with the general public and must always maintain the highest reputation), and have decided to dress your tellers in uniforms. If you have both male and female tellers, their uniforms should not be exactly the same. For a bank in the Midwest, I found that if the women wore light blue uniforms with dark blue lapels and dark blue stitching, and the men simply reversed the color, it worked very well.

Once you have dressed your tellers, most uniform companies will try to persuade you to do the same with your bank officers. This is not normally a good idea, for while a uniform will usually increase the authority of a teller, it will decrease the authority of any man whom the public is conditioned to seeing in a standard business suit, shirt and tie. It will severely decrease the authority of any man who heretofore wore the *right* suit, shirt and tie.

When you buy uniforms, do not buy them for every branch at once. Test several types in selected offices until you are sure that the uniforms are helpful, and until you have settled on the right uniforms.

The cheapest uniform is not always best, although many of the highly competitive uniform companies will try to convince you that they can do the same thing for you cheaper than the next fellow. And he'll show you how he uses exactly the same material as his more expensive competitor. What he won't show you is that his dyes may be harsher and his tailoring sloppier.

And that several dollars difference in the cost of the uniforms may well be the difference between lower-middle-class uniforms and upper-middle-class uniforms.

In short, I advise you to test uniforms before buying them; buy them from reputable dealers, and then buy them in limited numbers and test them as best you can. Think not only of how long the uniform will wear and how it will look on the employee, but what message it will say to every client or customer of your corporation that employee will meet.

THE LESSON FOR EXECUTIVES

I suspect that many executives reading the previous pages on uniforms have been saying to themselves, "Well, that's pretty boring and means nothing to me personally." Yes, putting uniforms on guards is not glamorous, but it is not unimportant to you personally because, now that you have an idea of how to choose uniforms for others, possibly you can choose uniforms for yourself.

Yes, a uniform—because, as I've hinted earlier—virtually every businessman in this country, whether he be the chairman of the board or the trainee right out of college, wears a uniform. These uniforms vary from industry to industry, from location to location, from company to company, but they exist and they dominate your scene—and they are uniforms.

In addition to being bored with the preceding, some executives have probably been saying, "Here's another fashion consultant picking on us, telling us we don't know what we're doing, that we should wear something we don't think is right."

That's not true.

I don't think most executives know what they are doing with employee uniforms, because that's not their business. Most executives do have very good ideas about office management, productivity and profit; that's why they are executives.

And over a period of years, they have developed what I refer to as executive instinct, which means that they often do the right things without sometimes knowing the reasons why. One of the right things that executives have been doing for years is dressing themselves in a very specific way, and persuading their employees, directly or by indirect pressure or nudging, to do the same. Until now, however, when some disgruntled employee has asked why he must wear a suit, shirt and tie to work, the executive has had to fall back on the answer, "Because I say so." And most of those executives have been accused of being medieval and backward and out of date.

HOW TO PERSUADE EMPLOYEES TO DRESS CORRECTLY

I will now give every executive the ammunition he needs to answer such questions. You no longer have to sound arbitrary because I have done the necessary research to prove that your instincts are not only correct but profitable to you and your employees.

My research shows without question that subordinates work harder and longer for bosses who dress in upper-middle-class, authority garments. It also proves that company loyalty is based on a sense of security, and that sense of security depends on the concept of their company that employees constantly carry in their heads. If you work for General Motors or IBM or any of the other giants, the concept of the company is predetermined. But if you work for any one of the tens of thousands of smaller corporations, the concept of the company will be based on the size of the building or the offices that people work in, and on their picture of everyone in the company who outranks them.

To the man pushing a broom, his concept of the company comes from everyone who has a desk; to the man who has a desk, it comes from everyone with an office; to everyone with an office, it comes from every corporate officer.

If company loyalty does not extend down to the lowest employee, then the corporation is not functioning at ultimate capacity. And it is only realistic to keep in mind that an executive's ability is of no meaning to the elevator operator who takes that executive downstairs at night. Yet that elevator operator's concept of the top executives is important to the corporation because his loyalty is an asset and because the elevator operator looks to the company to protect him. If an executive of the company looks as if he is stupid or unimportant, then the elevator operator cannot believe in the importance of the company or the value of its protection and cannot give it his loyalty.

IT'S NOT WHO YOU SEE—IT'S WHO SEES YOU

This kicks a hole in the argument of some executives who say, "Look, I know I'm a vice president of the company, but I work off in a corner and really never see anyone, so I can dress as I choose, and not hurt anything." Wrong! It's not whether the executive sees anyone, it's whether anyone sees him. Because everyone in the company will know that he is a vice president, and their concept of the corporation will partially depend on how he appears before them.

Let me illustrate the importance of dress codes with a rather strange story. In Philadelphia I was once consulting with a bank about its uniforms. Banks do not like to publicize this, but a tremendous amount of employee embezzlement goes on that the public never hears about, because the culprits are prosecuted very quietly or not at all. While I was at this bank, they had hired a psychologist to talk to some of their thieves to try and find out why they did it. He and I and several of the bank's executives were having lunch one day, and the joke around the table was that maybe clothing had some effect. One of the executives said that the only clothing that could have an effect would be striped prison uniforms, and we all laughed, and I forgot about it.

About four months later, I was called back to the bank to determine a proper dress code because the psychologist had interviewed some forty or fifty men who had stolen from a number of banks and had made a remarkable discovery. He asked if they were sorry; and most of them were only sorry they got caught. He asked them why they held that attitude. After all, the attitude was not so bizarre, but it was strange that the thieves would verbalize it.

Almost to a man, the thieves said because the bank had cheated them! Typically, they said: "I came to work for years and years and worked hard and obeyed the rules. I wore a white shirt and tie; I did everything they told me, everything you're supposed to do if you want to advance, and I didn't make it. Then these young punks came in with their long hair and mod shirts and they were promoted over me." All of the thieves saw this as a tremendous insult, had absolutely no remorse about sticking their hands in the till and were raging with resentment and didn't care who knew it.

At higher levels of corporations, this inclination, usually expressed in less drastic form, is called middle-management syndrome. I would not enforce strict dress codes in all corporations, but I did learn from the bank psychologist's study that if I had a business where people were handling my money or had access to it, I would enforce the strictest dress code imaginable. For every employee.

Another reason for adopting dress codes is that I can statistically prove that men make moral judgments of other men based on how they are dressed, and they make the same judgments of companies depending on the appearance of their employees. This is particularly true of the sales force representing the company in the field, but it is also true of the office staff visible to any visitor while walking to the president's office.

HOW TO SELL EXECUTIVES ON DRESS CODES

Now I hear you say, "Fine. We agree that dress codes are important and that dress codes start with executives. But how do you get an executive to observe them? What happens if he fights back?"

Well, frankly, I think that most men who are far enough up

223

the ladder are career-oriented enough to deal with the very sensible argument that the way they dress is part of their job, and is in fact part of what they are being paid for. One of the basic elements of leadership is example, and they must set a good example for the other employees.

In most cases, you can let it go at that, and your problems will be solved. If not, then you may be more specific and give them some other reasons that will encourage them even more. One is that the executive who dresses in conservative, upper-middle-class garments is far more likely to succeed than the man who dresses otherwise. It's a fact: Over 95 percent of the successful, important men in this country dress in conservative, upper-middle-class clothing.

Another reason: Any executive dressed in this manner will find it far more easy to deal with other executives as well as subordinates, both in and outside his own company. Most executives come from upper-middle-class backgrounds, and people from upper-middle-class backgrounds tend to distrust— even though perhaps not consciously—anyone who looks as if he comes from a lower-class background. This is true of all levels of society; lower-middle-class people tend to distrust other lower-middle-class people. And one of the chief determinants of class in the eyes of the beholder is dress. Any executive who decides not to wear the uniform of his position may still be in the race, but he's carrying extra weight, and although he may win, he will be working against a needless handicap.

HOW TO ENFORCE DRESS CODES TACTFULLY

I will come back to the specific clothing needs of the man at the top and the man who wishes to get there, but first I want to nail down the importance of the corporate dress code and how to make it work.

Once executives understand that corporate dress codes must start with them, they will enforce dress codes on the people below them. Most executives are right to set such codes, but wrong in the methods they use and the controls they apply.

To establish dress codes for top- and middle-management people, the rules are simple. Don't hire them if they are not dressed correctly when interviewed; if they deviate from the acceptable manner of dress after they are hired, tell them.

For those in authority positions below that level—and in this case "authority position" means any employee who has other employees reporting directly to him—there are several basic methods. The best, most obvious and still the most subtle is example. It will bring around most employees who possess a sense of responsibility. The recalcitrants should simply be informed, either directly or indirectly, that they are in positions of authority, and people in positions of authority in the company are expected to adhere to certain dress codes. They are expected to do so because research has indicated that companies with dress codes do better than companies that don't have them.

This is, in fact, true. A stockbroker friend of mine, at my behest, some years ago analyzed the stocks of companies with known dress codes and determined that by investing in a certain group of companies with very strict dress codes, as opposed to those in the same business without dress codes, an investor, for the period of time of his study, earned three dollars for every one he would have made on the companies with no dress codes.

Establishing and controlling the dress codes of general employees, those without authority over others, is a delicate matter, and three levels of employees are involved.

First, there is the employee whose appearance will not make any difference to the corporation no matter what he wears. Although all employees are part of their co-employees' environment and their clothing will have some effect, the indicators are not presently strong enough to put, say, line workers in an automobile plant in uniforms. I would leave this type of employee's dress to himself. It will be cheaper for him, and not harm the corporate efficiency to any statistically valid degree.

WHEN YOU CARRY THE COMPANY FLAG

The second type of general employee is the employee who creates a public image for the corporation. These fall into various categories, from the repairman who goes out to fix appliances, to airline ticket agents and stewardesses, to bank tellers —in other words any employee not in an authority position over other employees who must represent your company before the general public, regardless of capacity.

The proper uniform for such employees generally creates a positive reaction, but in each case, the need and the uniform should be measured specifically. When we speak of uniforms for such employees, it should be recognized that a uniform does not have to be what is traditionally thought of as a rigidly standardized, almost military-style uniform. The only necessity is consistency and coordination between the uniforms of all employees of the same sex. Automobile dealers, as I have already mentioned, have successfully dressed their salesmen in gray pants, blue blazers with company emblems on the breast pockets, and derivations of the club tie bearing the company logo. Such uniform-looks are highly effective, although they are not generally perceived as being uniforms.

The third category of general employee is the semipublic employee, the typical office worker. The office is quite definitely a visual segment in the corporate image, and is the element most often seen by visiting businessmen, clients or customers. It is essential for office efficiency that certain mandatory dress codes be maintained and there are two ways to get them started.

The simplest (and the easiest to adopt) is a written dress code posted on bulletin boards, but I do not believe this is appropriate in most cases. It creates more problems than it solves. It gives the company an impression of being stiff-necked, intransigent and an intruder on employee privacy, which is neither good employee relations nor good public relations. It also creates the problem of having affluent fifty-five-year-old male executives with absolutely no notion of fashion telling nineteen-year-old young women what to wear. This is ridiculous, and it never works. Most fathers of nineteen-year-old girls can tell you that do not approve of their daughters' dress, but they wouldn't dare interfere with it either. Women in this group, particularly those who are young and unmarried, will often pack up and leave rather than obey written dress codes.

If you want and need good secretarial and office help, you had best not step too heavily on their toes.

HOW TO SPREAD WORD ABOUT UNWRITTEN DRESS CODES

I believe in an *unwritten* dress code set largely by example and sound psychology. Male employees can be told rather specifically, if necessary, that suits, shirts and ties are required; this is not an unreasonable request. Beyond this, subtle ways exist for dealing with any problems of weird colors, patterns and styles, and platform shoes, etc.—God only knows what will be the clothing rage tomorrow.

Making a gift of this book to any employee with a look-successful problem may be helpful. If that doesn't work, or you don't want to give a book to a clerk who has no chance at the executive suite or even a management position, then it is possible to affect him through inference. Just make sure that everyone else in his immediate environment is wearing the proper attire. This will fail in only very few cases. Generally men in the office do not create major problems in their dress. If you have those who do continue to have a problem simply mention it to them as diplomatically as possible. They'll get the message.

HOW TO SET DRESS CODES FOR WOMEN EMPLOYEES

The major problems are created by women, for two reasons. They look upon clothing as an extension of their personalities, and to let someone else mandate their clothing is considered by them to be a surrender of part of themselves. Secondly, their concept of what is beautiful and good in clothing is, as I said at the outset of this book, diametrically opposed to the male concept of those qualities. For the same reason that wives should not generally choose their husbands' clothing, neither can male executives choose the clothing for women who do not feel comfortable in what would be chosen. (By the way, fifty-five-year-old female executives are no better or only slightly better qualified to choose the clothing for young female employees than are their male counterparts.)

The dress code for female employees had best be openly spelled out to the women when they are hired. The code should state that they should be neat, clean and appropriately attired. Any item such as a skirt that is too short (and I would *not* try to define in advance what is too short) or extreme makeup will be brought to their individual attention, with the expectation that it will be corrected. If the rules are kept general and ambiguous, they should arouse no hostility among female job applicants.

The next step is to have several female executives, as close as possible in age to that of the average employee, single out a few of the female employees to attend seminars directed by experts (some of the cosmetic companies would undoubtedly be delighted to provide the experts) on grooming and corporate dress. As an incentive to the women, the experts might offer hair and makeup tips in short courses that can be conducted at lunch or after work. But their basic function, to be worked out in advance, is for them to propagandize the female employees to wear exactly what you want them to wear, what would be in their best interests to wear, and at the same time, the information would not be mandated. It would be coated in the sugar pill of a basic beauty course.

At the end of the seminars, there should be a consensus period in which the general rules for office dress should be defined. If possible, publish as much as you can about the seminars and consensus in the company house organ. The plan is sensible, subtle and I have used it successfully for companies for years.

Trying to set absolute, intransigent rules is ridiculous; it does more harm than good. What happens if you get another mini-skirt craze? Or if makeup in general becomes extremely bizarre? You have no choice but to live with it. And if next year women decide to wear bones in their noses, fellows, there's absolutely nothing you can do about it, but accept it and hope that the bones are tasteful.

I have not covered the dress codes for female executives or career women because, quite frankly, the phenomenon is so complex that it requires a separate book to cover the subject adequately.

16.

DRESSING SUCCESSFULLY FOR JOB INTERVIEWS AND A NEW JOB

Before any executive can execute anything, he must have a job. He will have a better chance for a better job at a higher salary if he learns to use clothing as a business tool beginning with his initial job interview. The rules that apply to clothing and job interviews break down into various levels.

For upper-level industry and government positions, where the applicant is assuredly going to be interviewed by ultra-sophisticated, upper-middle-class (in both background and income) heads of corporations or government, he must have several appropriate suits, because he will go through a series of interviews and should never repeat what he is wearing during the course of these meetings.

Every item of clothing and every accessory must be conservative, traditional and conventional. All items should be elegant and costly and perfectly coordinated. Men who are interviewing for such positions can spot the difference between a $200 suit and a $500 suit at a glance, and while the $200 suit may be perfectly acceptable once you have the job, the $500 one will be a good investment in helping you get it. Please understand that this advice only applies to those men who are qualified and seeking jobs in a salary range of $100,000 a year or above, or for men seeking government jobs of great power and prestige. The $35,000 a year executive or the middle-level government bureaucrat who wears $500 suits will be regarded as reckless with his own money and will arouse suspicion that he won't be very thrifty with anyone else's money either.

Most men aiming at such positions really do not need me to tell them how to dress; if they don't know how to do it by the time they have reached the point of interviews of that caliber they will probably never learn. I have found, however, that they invariably make one mistake, particularly when they must travel to the interview, and that is they go to the interview directly from the plane in their traveling clothes. Don't! Always fly in the night before; take—but do not wear—your best suit, and have it pressed at the hotel.

The rules for top-level positions in smaller companies and middle-management positions in the larger ones are virtually the same as for the top-management men. You will still need several separate and distinctly different outfits, but they need not be so expensive. If the job you are going for is outside one of the major, relatively sophisticated large cities, then you must be careful, because you could be faced with several types of executives making personnel decisions.

The first is the man from a lower-middle-class background, who doesn't know how to dress himself, and who looks at anyone who does dress well as a smartass big-city boy. He will prejudge you on the basis of your clothing—in a reverse way. It's called lower-class snobbery.

The other type of executive is the sophisticated man who may be stuck in the sticks, but who knows clothing, and flies to New York to buy his Gucci shoes and $25 Bergdorf Goodman ties several times a year.

The first man will not hire you if you come on too slick, and the second man will not hire you unless you evidence the same awareness of clothing that he has.

If you know in advance whom you will be dealing with, your problems are decreased. If you do not, I always suggest that on the first interview, you wear a good solid-blue suit, a white shirt and a conservative, nondescript tie. When you get there, look around carefully, and find out whom you are to be dealing with. If you are to be dealing with other men you are to meet after the first interview, ask about their backgrounds. If they sound upper-middle-class, dress accordingly. If they sound lower-middle-class, do the same.

THE BASIC JOB-SEEKERS WARDROBE

The four suits I recommend for all men seeking upper- and middle-level positions are: that very conservative, dark blue suit for the first time in; a conservative, solid-gray suit; a conservative pinstripe suit, preferably with a vest, in either dark blue or dark gray (this being your most powerful, most authoritative suit, it should be reserved for wear with the most important man you must see); and, finally, a plaid suit for wear if you find the men less conservative in their dress than your other three suits.

Your shirts should be the standard white or pale blue solids, but you should have a good selection of ties. In Middle America, the traditional rep is acceptable to almost everyone. But just by changing your tie, you drastically change your image. Wearing the expensive, small-patterned, Daddy-went-to-Yale, Ivy League tie, you are saying that you are from a definite upper-middle-class background. And you wouldn't want to wear that in an interview with the executive from the lower-middle-class background whom you will only make uncomfortable by appearing better than he is. Likewise, the Pucci tie or any other expensive, wildly patterned or brightly colored designer tie is going to say that you are very hip and with-it, and that tie should be avoided for any industries except the glamour enterprises, where it is expected.

For the man seeking intermediate or future management positions, several conservative suits are sufficient, and they need not be expensive as long as they are well cut and well tailored. But it is essential that these be in keeping with the upper-middle-class patterns and colors outlined in previous chapters.

Interviews for these positions also usually go through several stages. The first is the screening stage where you will meet one or two of the people you will be working directly with or for. Then there is what is commonly referred to as the courtesy call on the top man. That's what it's called, but very often, that is not what it is. Instead, the top man has said to his subordinates, you select several men whom you think are qualified, and then I'll see them and make the final decision.

You must be very wary of such "courtesy calls." You should wear your best, most conservative garments, and you should conduct yourself in an almost formal manner. Regardless of whether he's actually going to be making the decision, he's a busy man, and you're not going to be in his office long. And the clothing you wear and the personality you display in those few minutes are going to frame his decision to a considerable degree.

IF YOU'RE JUST OUT OF COLLEGE

What about the young man right out of college going for his first or second interview?

Usually, his financial resources are limited and his wardrobe suffers accordingly. But large wardrobes, or even expensive wardrobes, are not the issue. The right colors, patterns and styles are. If this man has only one good suit, it should be a dark blue solid. If he can afford a second, it should be a gray pinstripe, preferably with vest. With those two, and appropriate shirts and ties, he should be able to get through most interviews.

If you land your position, your natural inclination is to take your newfound security and income and start buying stereos and sports cars and start dating expensive ladies. Don't fall for those temptations until you have an adequate wardrobe, even if you have to borrow to get it. I'll tell you why. You may think that your first few years of working are basically unimportant, but the exact opposite is true. In most corporations, you are being watched and tracked, and you are going to be routed in certain directions. Whether or not you are to be routed in directions that lead to upper management and success will depend on intelligence, ability and personality, obviously. But it will also depend to a great extent on how you dress.

I know many of the men who make these decisions. I know what they say, and I know what they think. And I know that clothing is an important, if not crucial, element in their decisions. If you do not believe me, go back and read the questions I put to 100 of these men on page 28.

They are not being unreasonable when they start tracking you at age twenty-four; they are being practical. They want their executives to be approximately forty-two years old and to have gone through a number of work experiences before they reach that age. If they don't start early, they won't make it. And if they don't dress correctly, they won't get started.

WHAT ARE THEY WEARING ALL AROUND YOU?

If you are a young man about to begin accumulating a business wardrobe, I suggest several specific steps before you buy a single item. The first is to undertake a general industry orientation. This simply means that in your chosen industry in your area, you should look at the dress habits of as many executives as you can see—at least twenty or thirty. Number them, and write them down. Eliminate the several most conservative, and the several most flamboyant from your list. You now should have a realistic range in which the successful men in your industry dress. If you position yourself in the top third from a conservative point of view, and in the top third in terms of neatness, tailoring and coordination, you will find yourself in a most advantageous position.

The most important orientation, of course, is in your own office. Here you should look at all men above you, all who have jobs you would like to have, all who are going to be making the career decisions about you, and, based on what these men are wearing, determine your own clothing goals. There is, by the way, no reason why you cannot dress better than your boss, as long as you do not make him look like a slob by comparison.

Once you have determined both the general industry and office standards of dress, you should have a solid idea of the acceptable range for successful dress. There is one additional range and that concerns your own physical and emotional characteristics. For this information, I would refer you back to Chapter 7, since that information is as relevant to corporate executives as it is to salesmen.

HOW CLOTHES CAN MAKE YOU MORE LIKEABLE

To re-emphasize: The overriding essential of all corporate business clothing is that it establish power and authority. If you can accomplish nothing else, presenting yourself as a person who is capable of the job he wants or has been given is an acceptable goal. There is one other prime element: whether other people like you, and certain clothing elements tend to make a man more likeable. Sounds crazy? I'm sorry, but I've got the research to show I'm right. Solid suits, for example, make a man more likeable than pinstripe suits, although pinstripe suits make him more authoritative. Men are more likeable by the upper-middle class in gray suits, more likeable by the lower-middle class in blue suits.

Combinations that increase likeability are gray suits with pale blue shirts and maroon solid or rep ties or beige suits with blue shirts. Pale yellow shirts with dark blue suits tend to have the same effect. Soft beige and soft browns are the best colors for plaid patterns if likeability is the goal. Anything that is too authoritative, too gaudy or too sharply contrasted creates opposite effects.

Any clothing that reminds the viewer of his youth creates a pleasing effect, and makes the wearer more likeable to the viewer. For example, if your boss is thirty-eight, he would be quite amenable to button-down collar shirts, end-on-end shirts and rep ties, because those were worn during his youth. If you don't have a personality that makes you immediately likeable, I would suggest that you avoid black suits, avoid lavender or pink shirts, avoid any type of purple, avoid small-patterned ties and avoid any strong clash in either the colors or the lines of your clothing. I also suggest that men with severe personality problems avoid the white shirt because it works for everyone except the man with a terrible personality.

WHY VIRTUE ISN'T EVERYTHING

Many men believe that men receive promotions in business due to their efficiency, reliability and hard work, but this is not always true, not even for the boss's son. More often than not, it is the *semblance* of these qualities that helps success along, rather than the reality of them. To create the look of these qualities, you, your desk and your office must be as neat and precise as possible. Your clothing must always be perfectly coordinated, in upper-middle-class patterns and colors. You should wear pinstripe suits, white shirts, conservative ties. Never wear loud or gaudy colors. If you work in an office where men take off their suit jackets, then take off yours and roll up your shirt sleeves; this creates the impression of hard work.

If you are permitted to decorate and arrange your office, then you should read and follow the advice in Chapter 13, because a properly decorated and arranged office can help in the creation of this image.

17.

MAKING YOUR CLOTHES FIT
THE OCCASION

The advice I have given on corporate clothing thus far applies to everyone or to particular individuals in particular situations. But the truly sophisticated executive is the man who realizes that he must come on as a different person on different occasions and must dress accordingly.

Use your clothing to help you fit the situation.

Although self-analysis is quite difficult for most people, we must recognize that some of us are just bloody dull. If you are, you can appear to be more lively simply by brightening your clothing. If you are too flamboyant, you can tone this image down by dressing in the most conservative manner possible. If you look as if you are too young for the position you hold, you can dress in the manner of an older man. If you're in a business dominated by men younger than you, you can break all my rules, wear European-cut suits and designer ties, and completely change your image. Although this breaks all my rules, it does adhere to the most formidable one: *Always use clothing as a tool.*

To apply this idea to specific situations, let us say that the average executive's week is divided as follows: On Monday, he meets with the president or chairman of the board. On that day he should dress extremely authoritatively and conservatively. On the second day, he meets with department heads, and should dress approximately the same. The third day he spends with his staff, and in order to maintain his working relationship with these people, he should soften his look slightly, with lighter colors, less contrast, none of the high-authority garments.

On the fourth day, he is seeing an executive of another major corporation and should wear clothing equal to that worn by the man he is going to see. On the fifth day, he goes to see an executive of a minor corporation, and since he doesn't want to overwhelm this man (or come on like the same conservative old stick in the mud that everyone in his corporation is supposed to be), he softens his appearance, brightens it a bit and wears a paisley tie.

This executive would truly be using clothing as a tool, and although his adjustments would be subtle, they would tremendously effect his psychological relationships with those with whom he came in contact.

Several other situations are becoming more and more common to executives for which very definite rules must be followed. The most important of these arrives when an executive is called upon to speak from a stage. For my own clients, I have a rather complicated set of rules, but then I usually know the purpose for which they are going to be on stage, and I can be quite specific in my advice. For this book, I have simplified the rules to fit more general situations.

The first rule for stage appearances is not to fall into yourself and make yourself invisible. No matter what other considerations you must face, you must be seen in order to command attention. If you go on stage in a light blue suit, a light blue shirt and a light blue tie, you will appear as a washed-out blue blob. People won't look at you. They are unlikely to listen to you, and you will be extremely ineffective. Forget any considerations of your position, authority or size on the stage. You must appear as a crisp definition of form. The dark blue suit with white shirt and dark blue tie is probably the best stagewear possible, since it is crisp, with high contrast, and makes any man stand out.

The second rule on the stage is not to fall into the background. This, of course, requires some prior knowledge of the background color against which you will appear. Whatever that background color is, make sure that you wear something to make you stand out from it. Incidentally, if your company has its own auditorium, and it has a curtained backdrop, as most do, buy a maroon curtain. No man will be wearing a maroon suit, and almost every color of acceptable suit will stand out against it. If you ever must get on a stage where you would be falling into the background, take off your suit jacket, regardless of the occasion. There's nothing else you can do; it is much better to look inappropriate than to have the audience ignore what you say.

Many men going on stage forget that distance changes perspectives, and this is particularly bothersome if the speaker is wearing coordinated small patterns. Let's say you are wearing a solid dark blue suit with a fine orange stripe, a dark blue pinstripe shirt that picks up the suit and a tie that is predominantly orange with a small blue pattern that ties the look together. Up close, it could be a tricky but perfectly coordinated outfit. But from fifteen or twenty feet away, you're going to look like a man in a conservative solid blue suit, conservative pinstripe shirt and a garish orange tie that is totally inappropriate with such a conservative outfit. So do remember: Unless your clothing looks crisply defined and well-coordinated from a distance, it is detrimental to wear on a stage.

Some patterns that are acceptable at close range can have a blinding effect from a distance. I remember attending a speech once where the speaker was wearing a blue checked suit. Up close, it wasn't too bad, but from the audience he looked like an angry, undulating ocean, and it was hard to look at him without getting seasick. So be very careful of odd patterns.

As I have said, the best clothing to wear on stage is a dark blue or dark gray solid suit; a white or very pale solid shirt; and a strong tie that picks up the color of the suit. Pinstripes are generally not advisable because the stripes can play games with people's eyes at a distance.

If you follow the above rules, you should be able to hold your own on stage, provided you know how to use a microphone, which most executives don't, but that's not my business.

The great stage of our society is, naturally, the television tube, and every now and then executives are called upon to appear on television. A while back, when the stock market was plunging, executives were appearing on television in droves trying to talk the American public into putting money into the market. They were largely unsuccessful for a variety of reasons, but one of those reasons was that they created a terrible personal impression. They did not even know the basic rules, which I shall herewith provide.

If a corporation must present itself on television for any reason, it should have select executives for this purpose. A large percentage of the television audience is women, and they like tall, handsome guys. They could care less about the president of the company. So choose a man for his appearance, affability and verbal smoothness.

This tall, handsome paragon of virtue should not wear stripes on television. Although television experts will tell you differently, I tell you that striped suits and shirts, unless the lighting is perfect, will tend to run. You can never go wrong wearing three solids on television, if they're well coordinated. Just don't wear a solid white shirt; there are technical limitations even for color cameras, and the shirt will invariably come out looking dingy to the folks at home. I suggest that on television you not wear a gray suit, since it is primarily positive only with the upper-middle class and your audience will be from all classes. The blue suit is the safe suit. The pale blue solid shirt (which will look white) is the safe shirt. Do not wear ties with small patterns. If reception is bad at home, the patterns will tend to jump and undulate, and people will not be able to watch you; if they are not watching, they won't be listening.

Many television experts do not know these things because they are accustomed to watching studio monitors, and on studio monitors, reception is perfect. But that has very little to do with what is being seen in the real world, where a combination of factors can give all sorts of reception trouble. So do wear solids if you can.

Since a large percentage of the audience is going to be women, and women are turned off by traditional clothing, you should avoid such conservative attire as the pinstripe suit, the rep tie and button-down collar shirts for that reason. Although every executive should have a short haircut, the exception is your man who must go on television. His hair should be up-to-date and styled. Don't forget that women never say that a man doesn't dress well; they say he doesn't know how to dress well, and if you don't dress well in their eyes, you're considered stupid in other ways, too. When you go on television, don't make the mistake of thinking that your audience is composed of people like you—other corporate executives—because if you dress for them and talk to them, you'll blow it every time.

When I consult with major corporations, I generally suggest that they designate two executives for television appearances—one to handle general problems and announcements and one to handle disasters, if disasters are possible in your business. For example, if you manufacture or sell school buses, one of those buses is going to be in an accident someday. And if you're questioned about it on television, you must not only *be* unhappy about it; you've got to *look* unhappy.

There are specific rules for handling disasters on television. The corporate spokesman should be fifty-fivish and distinguished. He should be dressed in a solid dark blue suit, a pale blue solid shirt and a solid maroon tie. This will enable him to come on, say he's sorry, and look sorry.

Let's take another type of disaster situation. Several years ago, one of the major aircraft manufacturers had large cost overruns on government contracts and wanted the American taxpayer to ante up the money. The president of the company went on television from behind his mammoth desk in his $400 suit, and explained why we should cover his losses. Then another executive in another $400 suit, wearing a white safety helmet that had never before been out of his closet, went down on the field to explain the cost overruns.

They thought they were getting their message across, but they were not. The message they were getting across was: "I'm a superior being and I'm in a superior class and you little peasants out there had better give me your money." The message that went to the congressmen who were laying in wait for the manufacturer was to go ahead and punch them in the head because these guys were obviously so harmless they couldn't even defend themselves.

What the company should have done was to use one man to cloak himself in science and patriotism. He should never have appeared in the office at all. He should have been interviewed down on the field wearing a white research scientist's smock and a slightly dirty, obviously used safety helmet. He should have picked up a screw and explained how that screw had to be able to withstand 9,000,000 vibrations a second, that it cost $3000 just to develop that one screw, and if we want better fighter planes that are safe for our young men to fly, we just must bite the bullet and spend the money. He probably would have been able to get his money with about half the trouble.

Going on television, then, means adapting one's appearance to the medium and using psychology.

THREE RULES WORTHY OF MACHIAVELLI

In addition to the foregoing, there are three other aspects of executive dress that every man should know:

1. In group situations, the effectiveness of any member of the group will be affected not only by his appearance but by that of all his associates. Super executive teams know this and plan not only the verbal parts but also the visual parts that their members are to play. For example, at a stockholders' meeting, the key

executives of the corporation should give forth the good news and be dressed similarly. Other executives should be assigned to tell the bad news and be dressed differently. This is not exactly like pitching the white hats of the cowboys against the black hats of the outlaws, but psychologically it is similar: probably the blue suits (good guys) versus the gray suits (bad guys). By visually as well as verbally separating the information process, the identification of the top executives with the positive aspects of how they are running the business is dramatically increased.

A more sophisticated way to apply this sense of association is to dress members of executive negotiating teams so that each member of the team visually fits the role he is to play.

The top man on the team should be immediately identifiable as the leader, merely by his expensive, elegant clothes. The second man, who is usually the spokesman, should look like a second man, but be visually associated in some way with the first, so no one can mistake for whom he is speaking. Any expert on the team should be dressed like an expert in his field; for instance, an accountant should wear a pinstripe suit. If there is to be a balloon man on the team—someone who is going to send up trial balloons to see if they will float—he should be visually disassociated from the leader of the team as long as he is floating trial balloons.

If one of the trial balloons catches on and is moving along in negotiation, on the day following its acceptance the balloon man should change his dress to bring him visually closer to the rest of the team. What can I tell you? It's a Machiavellian world, and whoever knows how to play the game wins.

2. Every executive should know that there is an absolute transfer of values between people and inanimate objects that they are identified with in advertising. If we see a man standing next to a machine, we automatically judge the quality of the machine by our judgment of the man. Therefore, if you let ad agency people choose beautiful individuals in lower-middle-class attire to stand next to your computer or tractor, the buying public may well be pleased by their appearance, but will think

less of your equipment. You should think a lot more about human dress the next time you get ready to spring for an expensive advertising campaign.

3. If you have a son, you are part of his environment, perhaps the most crucial part he will know. If you dress appropriately now and follow the rules I have set forth, then your son will not have to purchase the twentieth edition of this book twenty years from now.

FINALLY, TWO CRUCIAL MESSAGES

Throughout this book, but especially in this chapter, I have attempted to pack a tremendous amount of information into a small amount of space. I have tried to say something to almost every man to whom clothing is crucial for success, individually and/or corporately. If I have conveyed nothing other than the message that clothing should be used as a tool and as a weapon, then I have succeeded fully in my goal. If the reader has accepted my second message, that beauty is not the name of the game—efficiency is—then I am a perfectly happy man. If, by chance, the reader has received my third message—that some of my ideas can make him more effective and more successful—then I believe I have made a substantial contribution to the American business scene.

Acknowledgments

First and foremost, I would like to express special thanks to my friend and editor Tom Humber, whose professionalism made the difficult seem easy, and whose sense of style made the heavy seem light throughout *Dress for Success.*

The material in this book leans heavily on the genius of all the great researchers of motivation from Pavlov to Skinner, and to them I am grateful.

Acknowledgments

In addition, I am indebted to Dr. Ernest Carlson, who first introduced me to the use of the indirect-question survey. He helped me to develop the first true response questionnaire in this field, which enabled me to question hundreds of thousands instead of merely hundreds. This research forms the backbone of the book.

I also wish to express my gratitude to the management and staff, particularly the public relations department, of Bergdorf Goodman, for their assistance with the photography for this book. My thanks also go to the Men's Tie Foundation, which provided me with the best "how to tie a tie" pictures available.

Naturally, I owe special thanks to my clients, particularly the corporate clients, who not only supplied most of the cash needed for research, but also opened up their organizations to me. Without this opportunity to research corporate America from the inside, this book would be meaningless.

HOW TO GET YOUR PERSONAL DRESS FOR SUCCESS PROFILE

John T. Molloy, America's first wardrobe engineer, has been constructing personal profiles based on research for the leaders of government and industry for the past twenty-two years. He is now one of America's most sought after and highest paid corporate image consultants. He has taken his research and, with the help of a computer, he now makes it available to you.

The personal profile will give you advice based on your height, weight, coloring, position, company affiliation, geography, career goals, personal preferences, and other variables too numerous to mention. In addition, the program prints out a list of thirty-five suits, shirts, and ties in the order of their researched preference for your success. There are millions of possibilities in this section of the program alone. The advice is very specific and geared to you.

The advice is also geared to the changing environment we live in and is constantly updated. A new and expanded program is now available for $24.95 for either men or women.

Mr. John T. Molloy
P.O. Box 526
Wash-bridge Station
New York, NY 10033

Dear Mr. Molloy:

Please send me your new personalized DRESS FOR SUCCESS Questionnaire. I understand that 6 weeks after I return my filled-in questionnaire to you, I will receive my complete wardrobe profile.

_____ Enclosed is a check for $24.95 to cover the cost of the profile.

_____
Last Name (Please print)   First Name   Middle Initial

_____
Address   City   State   Zip